VICTORY
is my name

VICTORY
is my name

BOOK ONE:
The Burning Barrel

Victoria Chames

Other books by this author:

Inchworms: a chapbook,
Poems, Sketches, and Stories

More About This: Essays About Everything,
Metaphysical Thoughts & Questions of the Heart

A Space Between Rains: Love Poems About
Endings and Beginnings

©2020 by Victoria Chames. All rights reserved.
No part of this book may be reproduced without
prior written consent from author and publisher
except for quotations of brief passages used in
articles, critiques, or reviews.

ISBN: 978-0-9841730-9-9
V1-090925ngcx

Printed in the United States
Darkhorse Press
Oakland, California

For Jessie Baine Blakeman Long Vaughn
my Kentucky grandmother
1876-1952.
"The most cantankerous woman on earth"
who saved my life by loving me
when nobody else had the time.

TABLE OF CONTENTS

Preface and Introduction
Chapter 1: Killing Doves. 1
Chapter 2: Greensboro 9
Chapter 3: Mama Hill's House 25
Chapter 4: Beacon and Columbia 37
Chapter 5: East Side Avenue, Part 1 56
Chapter 6: My Granny Vaughn 72
Chapter 7: East Side Avenue, Part 2 85
Chapter 8: The Red Brick Apartment Building 96
Chapter 9: Stigall Street 113
Chapter 10: In My Mother's House 122
Chapter 11: Ann 128
Chapter 12: Austin 138
Chapter 13: Port Arthur 151
Chapter 14: New Haven 161
Chapter 15: Us 180
Chapter 16: Minneapolis. 196
Chapter 17: Jim and Joe. 212
Chapter 18: The Storefront. 228
Chapter 19: Freefall 238
Chapter 20: Keego Harbor 250

Preface: About The Book

Throughout the Victory Trilogy, the narrative is written in the voice and from the observing mind of the storyteller herself, first as a child, and later as an adult. The reader can only know what she knows and see what she sees.

There are poems and passages from a personal journal that chronicle events and feelings captured as they happen within the narrative. There are sometimes italicized paragraphs or sentences within the narrative text. These all mark inner shifts in consciousness of the storyteller, such as a vivid flash of memory, a silent thought, a dream, or a deeper insight. These are written in present-tense, and briefly step away from the narrative, which is always in past-tense and standard type-font. Inner shifts in consciousness like this are common to everyone in moments of reflection or daydreams. Hopefully this will be natural and easy for the reader to follow.

Few names have been changed, and only in cases where I felt privacy might be preferred by the person. In general only first names are used, and every event and person has been presented with dignity, discretion, and respect.

A memoir is the truth as the author felt and experienced it. Memoir is not history, so others who saw or participated in some of the same events may have had a different perspective, and so may remember them differently.

Uniquely the writing of memoir expresses the thoughts, feelings, and learning-path of the author, often with the purpose of honestly sharing personal truths that might benefit others on their own path in life as well. That is my hope and intention.

Introduction

The stories are not so much about my life as they are about the things I learned rightly or wrongly from living it, and the people who taught me. I needed to write about my birthmother, not just her history here on earth, but who this woman was whose body gave birth to mine, whom I never really knew and who never knew me.

For everyone, no matter what happens later in life, our earliest learnings from about age three to twelve take deep root in the new-forming brain and become our lifelong core-beliefs about how life works and who we're supposed to be. The most lasting voice in our lives is that shadowy inner one, because we will create the life we seek and have, out of these basic beliefs. We often unknowingly create a life we don't really want, based on untruths we accepted without question when we were very young.

I believe the hardest task of adulthood is discovering and unlearning our untruths, and reclaiming the authentic Self we were born to be. When our unrecognized untruths are finally revealed, we can begin to replace them with truths that fit us, and stop struggling to fit ourselves into someone else's template of what we should be. When we see our hidden limiting beliefs in the light of conscious awareness, we can begin to challenge, change, and heal them.

I carried into my lonely marriage some of the issues I had learned in childhood. From my birthmother, the role of the willing martyr. From my bullying older brother, the role of victim. Nobody told me how to stand up for myself, I was told "nice girls don't." I was bound to fall victim again and again, in another scenario, another time, another way.

Until one day I realized that *I didn't know how to fight*, and finally I knew that I had to learn how. Then, as I had often done as a child, I would dare the audacity to question and to challenge the unfair "rules for girls."

My birthmother Ann never did.

We left each other's lives when I was thirteen. I had a new life and I joyously left the old one behind. Events of both our lives would echo the history of abandonments of mothers and daughters going back three generations that I never knew of until just before my birthmother died.

I spent most of my young adulthood believing I had safely forgotten her, and denying my woundedness. Yet hidden emotional "unfinished business" still remained. This book insisted on returning to it, facing it, and finishing it. Then, it promised me, I would finally be able to forgive and be forgiven.

Making the storyteller the voice of the child, and later the woman she became was a new way of writing, and it surprised me. I'd never realized before how painful and baffling grown-up things like divorce and alcoholism are for a child until I returned to that time, looked down on all of it happening as if from a balcony over a stage, and listened for the simple words she spoke.

I wrote the book because it demanded to be written. It's the story of four strong women: my grandmother, my birthmother, my true Mother, and myself. I know more about my part of the story than theirs, and memory must always be imperfect and incomplete, but what I remember, I will share with you honestly, and hope to do justice to us all.

Chapter 1: Killing Doves

Before he got the gun, my brother could only torment me and small creatures with rocks and slingshots and spitwads, he couldn't really kill anything. Well nothing big anyway. Tommy liked to squish fat green caterpillars between two bricks, but that didn't need any skill. With the gun he figured he was a real big deal. It was a Daisy Special, pump-action BB rifle. I don't know where he got it from, if he stole it or what. Mama sure didn't have any money for stuff like that.

I was eleven going on twelve and Tommy was nearly fourteen and we'd just moved to East Side Avenue. That was when Mama and Daddy sort of stopped talking to each other. Mama got a new waitress job nights at the Diamond Horseshoe Bar and Grill. I don't think she liked it half as much as her old job at Mr. Joe Yee's Chinese and American Restaurant, but she said it paid more tips.

Tommy loved that BB-gun. He practiced shooting it every day and pretty soon he was a dead-eye shot. He shot at whiskey bottles and beer cans in the alley, and when he got pretty good, he started shooting birds. Not sparrows, they were too small to hit, but red cardinals, bluejays, and mockingbirds. I hated that he killed the pretty ones, but the mockingbirds even more, because they were my favorites. Mockingbirds are not beautiful. They're plain brownish-gray, but they're smart. They know how to imitate the songs of other birds, and they're the state bird of Texas.

Whenever Tommy shot one he would bring its little limp body and show it to me and try to make me cry. I would steel myself and pretend I didn't care, determined not to flinch. But at some point he would suddenly shove the thing at my face and I would jump back and shriek. Then he busted out laughing and swaggered off, snickering over his shoulder about what a big sissy I was.

One time Tommy and his buddies shot a whole bunch of doves. Mourning doves. There were lots of them all over the city of Dallas, like pigeons in New York I guess. Grownups thought they were a nuisance, but I thought they were sweet and I loved them. Every evening at twilight they would sit all in a row along the edges of the rooftops, cooing softly while the sun was going down.

The boys must have just picked them off like a shooting gallery. Tommy was so proud of himself, like he was the Great White Hunter in a Tarzan movie. He brought home his share of the kill for Granny to cook, and she did, too.

My granny had lived a long time. She grew up in Kentucky back in the days people killed things to eat. When I was little and we lived in North Carolina, it was Granny that wrung the neck of every Sunday-dinner rooster. Nobody else had the nerve to do it. She knew how to skin rabbits too, and cook possum. I don't think I ever ate any possum but I'm not sure. My brother didn't usually kill things to eat though. Mostly he did it for target practice.

Granny made Tommy pluck all the feathers off the little doves, leaving their sad pale bodies all naked and ashamed. Then she slit them open and cleaned out their tiny insides and washed and prepared them for the oven, just like all of this was okay. I watched from a distance. I used to watch Daddy clean the Sunday-dinner chickens when I was little, but now that I was eleven, I knew too much. I knew that the pretty little doves had got their innocent life taken from them for no reason. To eat them was so awful I couldn't even think of it.

Granny roasted them in the oven. It didn't take very long. When she brought them to the table, the dozen or so of them barely covered the plate. They looked like a heap of tiny corpses, tossed into a pile like in those old movies about World War II, the big war that was going on when I was born. There was no way on earth I was going to eat them, and all of a sudden I felt so sad for them. My face got hot and my eyes filled up with tears and I couldn't even say anything. I stood there for a minute and then I turned around and walked out of the kitchen, and out of the house.

Granny didn't call me back. She knew I was different from my brother, how things that made me cry made him laugh. As I went down the stairs, he jeered and laughed louder to make sure I'd hear him all the way to the bottom.

Outside, I kept on walking. I needed to get away from there until it was over. That meant I probably wouldn't get any dinner. There was a hungry ache in my stomach and a sad ache in my chest and another ache in my throat where it was clenched to keep from crying. The tears came anyway and flooded down my cheeks. I wiped my face with both hands and kept walking. I didn't care if anybody saw me.

The tears made the blue of sky and the green of summer blur together like watercolors. It didn't matter, I didn't need to see. I knew the way. I walked the ten blocks to Randall Park and climbed up my favorite easy tree.

I lay down on my stomach on a smooth broad branch for a long time. I watched the twilight drop down into the tops of the trees along the park's dark horizon, and I just let the tears flow as much as they wanted to. Nobody could see me now. Nobody could laugh at me.

When the sky was completely dark and the first stars began to come out, there was nothing to do but go back home. To be honest I felt more at home and more sheltered in my tree, but I was practical. I knew there was peanut butter and soft white bread in the pantry, and I knew I needed to eat.

Tommy was two years older and bigger than me and he had always picked on me for as long as I could remember. Since I was born, I guess. He would punch me, poke me, stick me with pins, burn me with matches, give me the one-knuckle shoulder-punch or the wrist Indian-burn, or shoot me with his slingshot or rubber bands or whatever was handy, any time he felt like it. He thought that was really funny. Usually he favored injuries that wouldn't show a bruise until the next day, so if I told Mama, he would just say, "She's crazy! I never even touched her!" And when he got caught with the weapon in his hand, he would say it was an accident. That was a lie, but he would smile his special smile for Mama with his face like an angel, and look so earnest with his dark Greek eyes like Daddy's, and she fell for it every time.

"He didn't mean to, honey, and he's sorry." She always said that. I tried to tell her, "Yes he did! He did mean to!" But she always believed him instead of me, and there he was behind her, sticking his tongue out at me, grinning because he got away with it again.

Most of the time he did it when nobody was near by, and when I yelled, "STOP IT!" Mama or Daddy would say,

"Tommy, quit picking on your sister." Like that was gonna do any good. He kept right on doing it, and I kept on saying "Stop it!" and pretty soon Daddy would holler:

"If I hear one more peep out of either one of you, I'm gonna come back there and whip the tar out of the both of you." He never did, but that left me at Tommy's mercy, and he didn't have any mercy.

I made myself a pledge and promise: *I will never be like him, no matter what. Boys are mean, and being stronger than somebody else makes mean people meaner. I will never be like that.*

Sometimes he made me go with him to the freight-train gravel yards late at night, mostly for somebody to show off to. We hid in the shadows near the frontage road and he chucked small pebbles at passing cars. With a quick whip of his arm, he could crack a windshield with the tiniest stone, so the driver would think it had been kicked up from the road. They never saw us hiding there in the dark.

I had to stand there and wait until he decided to go home. I could outrun him, but I couldn't outrun his pitching arm, which was deadly-accurate, especially with small stones or bits of broken glass, and when they hit, they stung. The times I got in trouble were usually times like that, when he made me go along with him on something I knew we shouldn't do.

I think my brother had a natural instinct for hunting. In Dallas where we lived, there wasn't much to hunt, but still he constantly practiced his skills. One day he was doing a jungle-warrior thing. He had made a javelin by sharpening the end of an old rake-handle. He was throwing it at made-up targets around the yard, and he decided to see how close he could come to the little blanket on the grass where I was playing with my doll. His first throw spiked the spear right through a corner of the blanket, pinning it to the ground. I hollered "STOP it!" He laughed at me.

He threw it some more times, and it dug up little chunks

of dirt and grass around me. He was getting pretty cocky. The next time he threw it, it stabbed right into my barefoot big toe. The spear balanced there, sticking up in the air for a long second or two, then it fell over with a clunk and a lot of dark blood gushed out of my toe. I screamed.

Tommy grabbed my arm and yanked me through the yard, up the stairs and through the kitchen to the bathroom, leaving a trail of little blood drops all along the way. He put my foot into the bathroom sink and ran the hot water on it. That hurt like heck, and I screamed again. The hole in my toe was bleeding all over the place and the hot water made it hurt worse and bleed more. I was yelling and Mama heard it and came to see what was going on.

When she looked in through the bathroom door, the sink was almost overflowing with the blood and water mixed together and it looked just like a sinkfull of blood. Mama's face went white as candle-wax and she staggered back for a second. I thought she was going to faint, but she didn't. Tommy started right in, talking fast:

"It was an accident! I didn't mean to do it... it was just... I was just practicing... It was an accident."

This time the "accident" needed a trip to the emergency room and stitches that Mama couldn't afford. But since it was an accident, as usual he didn't get punished. Maybe it *was* an accident this time; it could have been, I guess. Tommy always loved to take chances, push his luck. That's just the way he was.

My toe hurt something horrible. The ache went all the way up my leg and it lasted for a week. I had to keep my foot propped up so the throbbing wouldn't be so bad, but I got to stay home from school for two weeks. The rake-handle spear had cut through the tendon to the bone, and they had to sew some inside-things back together too. It healed up eventually with a diamond-shaped scar. After that, the toe was a little bit crooked, but that didn't slow me down for long.

At eleven I had legs like a grasshopper but I could run like a racehorse and pretend I was Man O' War, the magnificent thoroughbred. In my ordinary self I was small and weak and picked-on, but when I ran, I was fast and bold and splendid. Every time I ran, I went to that place in my mind where I was swift and strong, *and I became swift and strong*. And then absolutely nothing in the world could catch me. I was blazing and brilliant when I ran. That was my strength; that was my glory: I could *run*.

I ran through the neighborhood like a steeplechase horse in a British fox hunt, leaping gracefully over fences and hedges. I never felt so alive as I did when I was running. I ran barefoot everywhere, all summer long.

One time I was playing at the park and a storm came up. All of a sudden it started getting dark, and thick woolly grey clouds came rolling across the sky just like pulling up the blankets over your head. A rainstorm was coming. I figured I'd better go home.

In a few minutes the wind was whipping up really fierce and the trees were tossing and thrashing and there was a strange wonderful feeling in the air, like it was crackling with electricity. As I headed home, the raindrops started. Just a few at first, but big ones, plopped onto my forehead. It was a long way, so I decided to run.

The rain came down harder, and pretty soon there were torrents of it, thumping on the top of my head, splattering down my face and pelting my shoulders. I just kept on running. Streams of water were rushing through the gutters. I went splashing through them, pretending like I was a wild Mustang crossing raging rivers. The water felt cool and delicious on my bare feet.

Running in the rain was so joyful I could hardly stand it! It was like I didn't weigh anything, like I could almost fly! All around me the thunder boomed and rumbled, and bright threads of lightning streaked across the sky. The rain kept pouring down and spilling all of itself onto the earth like a huge gift. Everything smelled fresh and clean and the air was so alive. I ran through it all, and I felt so beautiful and wild.

I am the storm! I am fast as the wind! And nothing in the world can catch me!

Chapter 2: Greensboro

I got born in the ugliest month of the year on a Tuesday in the dark before dawn, and I nearly died doing it.

"You were what they called a blue-baby," Mama said. I asked her, "How could I be blue?" and she told me.

"Well, when you were born, you came sooner than we expected. With Granny's stroke and all, I guess I lost track of the due date. I felt the baby coming, just like when your brother was born. It was the dead of winter and bitter cold, and the time came. I called the doctor's office and the nurse told me to go to the hospital and he would meet me there, but something happened and he didn't get there. You started being born and he wasn't there yet."

I think I was six or seven when she told me the story. I didn't understand much of it, but I never forgot. One thing I learned was: being born blue is not a good thing.

"The doctor was late," Mama said, "so he called the hospital and told the nurses to hold my legs together so the baby wouldn't come, because if the baby was born before he got there, he wouldn't get the fee. So the two nurses did as they were told."

What? I was baffled at this.

"I fought 'em," Mama told me. "I wasn't going to let them do that – I knew it was time." She said the nurses tied her wrists to the table with leather straps and then they tried to strap her legs together. "I'm not a mean person," she said, "but I fought that time. I got one leg free and kicked one of the nurses in the head."

I couldn't even imagine that.

"They both backed up then, and you were born," she said. "When your little body came out, it was all splotchy and it was an unnatural grayish-blue color." I tried to picture that. It was ugly.

"The baby didn't cry. It didn't seem to be moving at all. I knew something was wrong. I remembered how much Tommy had kicked and hollered when he was born. The nurses snatched the baby and took it away to another room. I didn't even get to see if it was a boy or a girl. All I saw was that it was not pink and wiggling, and it was not making any sound. When they took it away, they just rushed out and left me there. I was so scared. I was afraid the baby was dead."

What? I was this ugly splotchy blue thing. I was not right. I was not like a baby should be, and she was calling me It.

She said when the doctor finally got there he was mad. He snapped at the nurses, "Clean her up!"

"I could smell the whiskey on his breath," Mama said, "even over the smell of blood and disinfectant in the delivery room. Then he just walked out," she said, "and the nurses went too. They all left me there. I was still bleeding from the birth, and the afterbirth was on the delivery table."

I didn't understand. I didn't know having a baby made you bleed, but before I could ask, she went on with the story.

"When the nurses came back, they were rough with me when they washed up the birth blood. They took me in a wheelchair to a room down the hall and put me in a bed."

She said she kept asking everybody, "Where is my baby? Is it okay?" And the nurses just answered, "The doctor will be in shortly" and then they left again.

"I could hear the voices of the nurses and the doctor down the hallway, but it sounded like they were miles away. I felt so weak, like I was floating underwater. I tried to get up, but I couldn't. Finally the nurses came back. They pumped my breasts, and they gave me a shot to make me sleep."

I think she must have been really scared, because she was bleeding, and because of the ugly blue thing that came out of her instead of the baby she expected.

"I was knocked out," she said, "so I don't know how long it was before they finally brought the baby to me. You were pink, and you were crying. I thanked God when I heard the baby crying."

I might have been a pale pink, she didn't say. But I was no longer blue, and I was alive. I was born "a darkhorse" she said. I came into this world against all the odds from the start, but I made it.

If I was a boy, they were going to name me Peter after Daddy's younger brother, or Jessie after Granny if I was a girl. Then Granny had a stroke, and I guess they thought her name might be bad luck, so I got the name of Daddy's father's sister who died at age eighteen from a broken heart because her father, my Daddy's grandfather, would not let her marry the young army officer she fell in love with. That was back in Greece. Ever since then her big-brother (my Daddy's father) wanted to name one of his children after the sister he loved, but he never did.

He ran away to be a sailor and worked on cargo ships on the ocean. That's how he came to America and married

Sophia, my Yaiya. She gave him four sons including my Daddy, but no daughters. I was the first girl grandchild, so the name at last chosen for me was the name that had been waiting for two generations: Victoria.

When I got old enough to understand, Yaiya told me, "There is a power in names." She said, "Your name is Victoria, this is a strong name. It means one who conquers. Your great aunt, you're named after her, she was beautiful but she was not strong. You must be strong." Yaiya's name is Sophia. It means wisdom.

My first weeks in the world, an old colored lady named Hattie took care of me. I saw a picture of her once. She was very skinny and wrinkled as a prune, but she had the face of a saint. In the picture she is sitting in a rocking chair, holding a tiny bundle of me in her arms. Mama said she always had to scold her for spoiling me.

Later there were babysitters who watched me and Tommy during the day, young girls who would work for low wages because there were so few jobs for colored girls except in the tobacco processing plants down by Winston-Salem.

"Tommy was a good baby," Mama said. "He was always happy and he hardly ever cried."

"I was a good baby too, wasn't I?

"Well, you were a nervous baby" she said, "You cried a lot. You threw your bottle out of the crib, so we used a Coca Cola bottle instead so it wouldn't break."

Tommy was two years old when I was born, and he didn't like me one bit. I was not welcome at all in his world. I was born fighting for my life from the minute I hit light and air and four days later, my brother tried to kill me.

He dumped a whole can of talcum powder into my face and down my throat. Somebody heard me choking and came just in time. They never scolded him for that. Years later Mama would laugh and tell about it for a cute little story.

"He must have seen me powdering her bottom when I changed her diaper, and he was just trying to help," she'd say, all proudly, like he was such a good boy. But he was not trying to help, and I learned early that the world was a dangerous place where I was an unwelcome intruder.

From the start, my brother was the boss of everything. He was the pretty one, Daddy's "chip off the old block" and Mama's precious angel. He had dark eyes and dark hair like Daddy. I was different, quiet and shy. I had Daddy's brown eyes but blonde hair. I wasn't as pretty as Tommy and I didn't look much like Daddy. I looked like Mama.

Granny's stroke made her blind and deaf and crippled and she couldn't even talk, but I was a little baby so I didn't know. By the time I was two years old, she had got her eyesight back and she could talk, but she was deaf for the rest of her life. She could walk again, not as good, but she was still the first one that got up in the morning and started the fire in the little pot-bellied stove in the corner of the kitchen. Then she came up and got me and brought me downstairs. When the rest of the family came down, Daddy sat at the kitchen table and read the newspaper. Mama and Tommy were there too. I ate my Cream of Wheat. Granny put butter and milk and sugar in it for me.

Our house was at the top of the hill near the courthouse. Our street had a half-dozen houses on both sides of it, then it ended at Mr. Jones's turnip field.

I had a little dog named Gingersnaps. I loved her so

much. She was a Manchester terrier, brown and black. She was very shy, and she had the prettiest brown eyes. She followed me everywhere. Sometimes Tommy pulled her ears and made her cry. She always ran away from him and tried to hide behind the kitchen door. She was my little friend and she was always right there next to me every minute. Then one day when I woke up she was gone. I looked all over. Mama saw me looking and she she had to tell me.

"I'm sorry Vickie, but Gingersnaps had to go away. She growled at Tommy, and we were afraid she might bite him."

"No! She wouldn't! She never would do that!" But it was no use. I asked Mama, "Where did she go? When is she coming back?" and my eyes were filling up with tears.

Mama said "She's not coming back, honey. She went to live on a farm where there are other dogs and cats she can play with, and she'll be happier there."

"No!" I said, *"No, she won't!"* But I could feel that little ache in my chest that told me it was too late.

I remember Greensboro, summer evenings, lightning bugs blinking in the dark, and the uneven wooden boards of our front porch that creaked with the rhythm of granny's rocking chair while she rocked me to sleep. From Granny's lap I looked up at the stars and the pale mysterious moon, and I felt so safe and happy. Then the next thing I knew, I woke up in my crib and it was morning.

I didn't know how to be afraid of anything. I had Granny and Mama and Daddy. They were always there, and I thought they always would be. The sun shone down so lovely and warm on the dust and crabgrass of the chicken yard and the smooth worn boards of the back porch, and that was beautiful enough for me.

Mama didn't work then. She was just Mama. Daddy worked for the Greensboro Police Department on the night patrol and in the daytime he was always working at his drafting table in the living room, studying something called Aeronautical Engineering. "It's the future for America," he said. I wandered around the living room behaving myself.

I liked to play with the telephone. It had a round flat wheel on the front of it with holes so you could put your finger into them and spin the dial around. I did this over and over because it made a nice little clickety noise I liked.

Sometimes the radio was on. I learned the songs and sang along. There was one that went "Round and round Hitler's grave, round and round we go... Gonna lay that fella down so he don't get up no more." I didn't know what that meant, but it had a cheerful tune, so I sang it sometimes when I was playing in the chicken yard.

It was wartime and the president was Mr. FDR. Daddy said it was hard-times, and that's why people like us had chickens in their backyards, so they could sell the eggs and some of the chickens for money. That winter Daddy had built a chicken coop out of scrap lumber and tar-paper and finally one day when it was almost summer, he brought home a big cardboard box full of sweet fuzzy yellow baby chicks. He put them into the chicken coop in the part where some light bulbs were, to keep them warm he said. They crowded together, all "cheep, cheep, cheeping." I think they were scared. They liked it though, and before too long they grew and started to look like real chickens, only smaller. When they got their grownup feathers, some of them were brown and some of them were white. Tommy chased them around the yard, yelling and poking a stick at them to make them flap and flutter like crazy.

Sunday was always my favorite day. Everybody was there: Mama and Daddy and me and Tommy and Granny. Everything was happy and the house was full of us. About the middle of the morning, Granny went out to the back yard and sat on the porch stoop until a likely-looking chicken came scratching and pecking nearby. Most times a rooster, because she said, "You don't need that many roosters." Then she grabbed him quick by the neck. If I was outside, I knew it was time for me to come in. From the kitchen I'd hear a squawk and then a clunk. She had wrung the neck of the unlucky rooster to kill it, and chopped its head off with the cleaver. Nobody else had the gumption to do that part, only Granny. Each time the deed was done, Tommy looked at her with a mixture of fear and awe.

Then she hung the rooster by its feet upside down from the porch rail so the blood could drain into a bucket while she pulled off the feathers. After that she washed the bucket and the cleaver with the garden hose, and then she brought the chicken inside.

I never saw that first part, or the chicken either until it was naked with no feathers, so my mind didn't make the connection that the chickens in the yard were the same ones on the table for which we gave thanks at Sunday dinner.

Daddy's part was next. I watched from my perch on the windowsill next to the sink. First he took all the innards out. He put his hand up the chicken's bottom and pulled out all kinds of stuff like a magician. It had never occurred to me before that there might be *things inside of things.*

After the chicken was cleaned and cut up in pieces, Mama powdered it with lots of flour and salt and pepper and then fried it up crisp and brown in crackling spattering hot grease in the big black iron skillet. Then with all the rest of it: mashed potatoes with giblet gravy, baby carrots, collard greens, buttermilk biscuits, and iced tea, Sunday dinner was a master piece, Daddy said.

For the rest of the week sometimes Granny cooked and sometimes Louise did. She was a colored girl fifteen years old. She did the washing and ironing and took care of Tommy and me during the day. She seemed like a grown-up to us, only more fun. We loved her; she read us comic books and secretly gave us potato chips and chewing gum and other treats we were not supposed to have.

She was a chubby girl and she had big buzooms. One time when Mama and Daddy were gone, Tommy asked her if she would show him one of her titties. She laughed, and when Louise laughed, every bit of her bounced up and down. It made you laugh too. She reached inside of her dress and pulled out one of her big brown buzooms so Tommy could see it. He squealed and laughed and jumped up and down. Louise was laughing at him, and pretty soon I was laughing too, and then we all were laughing. It was so silly. We never did tell Mama and Daddy about that.

Louise made wonderful desserts for us, molasses pecan pies, lemon meringue pies that made your lips curl just to think about it, and wild blackberry pies with basket-weave crust on top. Then while we all ate them, she went outside and sat on the back porch in the chicken yard. She couldn't eat any of that kind of food because she had the sugar-diabeet-tees. She sat there all by herself on the porch every time and cried. It made me sad. I wondered what this thing was, the sugar-diabeet-tees. It seemed so not-fair.

Sometimes on warm evenings, Tommy and I would get to stay up until dark and play in the front yard. There were lightning bugs sailing around in the dusk, but you couldn't see them until they blinked their little lights. Mama called them fireflies.

Tommy liked to catch them. I caught some too, though not as many. You had to snatch them right out of the air, quick, before they disappeared again. I held one in the palm of my hand and looked at it very carefully. I thought it was marvelous that they could make this little greenish-white light with their tails. Well really, it was the whole back half of their body that glowed. They could make it light up and then turn it off again. After I caught them and wondered about them, I let them go so they could fly off with their friends again.

Tommy put his into a jar so he could have a whole lot of them. One time he took one, and with his fingernails he pinched off the glowing part of its body and set that on his finger to show me. "Look!" He said, "I've got a diamond ring!"

The torn-off part was still glowing. I knew it wasn't a diamond ring, and now the rest of the lightning bug, the part he threw away, would die. It didn't seem right that something had to die just because it was pretty. I knew the others in the jar would die too unless he let them go. Sometimes he did.

Daddy was a policeman and I was proud. They help little kids who are lost and bring them home again, and they catch bad people and put them in jail. Every night before I went to bed, Daddy put on his uniform and his badge. My Daddy was a hero, and I wanted to be just like him. I'd seen cowboy movies where the sheriff had a silver badge and he brought justice to the town where he lived. My Daddy had a badge too.

Daddy had a pair of beautiful cowboy boots, black leather with white eagles on the front. He never wore them; they were in the back of the closet. When I found them one day, I stuck my legs into them and clomped around the house pretending I was a cowboy. I kept that up for a week.

Then one day Daddy brought home a pair of cowboy boots for Tommy, just his size. They didn't have eagles on them, but they were cowboy boots! I was so excited, and I said, "Ohhhh - Do I get to have cowboy boots too?"

"No, sweetheart," and he chuckled. "Cowboy boots are for boys."

Mama must have seen the puzzlement on my face because she said, "Vickie honey, you can have some ballet slippers. Wouldn't you like to have pretty ballet slippers?"

I stared at her. *What?* I looked at Daddy, and then I looked back at Mama again.

"No!" I said. "I don't want that! I want cowboy boots!"

Nobody even noticed how mean that was, to make me have ballet slippers instead of wonderful cowboy boots! Tommy didn't even care about cowboy boots, except because it made him specialler than me because he got to have what I wanted and I couldn't.

I begged for cowboy boots too, but it was no use. I started to cry, but that didn't do any good either. I said, "Please, please!" and I kept asking them why Tommy got to have what I wanted so much, but I couldn't have it too. The only answer I ever got was "Because, honey, cowboy boots are for boys."

Until then, I didn't know I was somebody less than my brother. I didn't know girls couldn't have what they wanted. I didn't know I wasn't supposed to want what I wanted, because I was a girl.

August came. It was a Sunday and I was wearing my green-and-white-checked dress that had a white ruffled pinafore to go with it. It was my best dress-up dress. I felt like the prettiest little girl in the world. I knew I wasn't, but that didn't matter, because I felt like I was.

It was hot and the front door was open for the breeze. All of a sudden there was a big commotion outside. I went to the screen door to look out and I could see people coming out of their houses across the street, shouting and looking toward our house and the vacant lot next door. Mama came hurrying into the living room and rushed right past me, out the door. I wanted to go too, but Granny grabbed my arm and pulled me back. She sat me down on the couch and brought me my crayons and a coloring book, so I did that. I could hear people yelling outside and cars on the street. Granny kept going to look out the front door, but every time I got up to look too, she sat me right back down again. I got curiouser and curiouser, especially when all the sirens came. After a long time, Mama came back. She picked me up and carried me outside. When I saw it, I started to cry.

The big empty field next door where I loved to play was all burnt black. The weeds and sunflowers and blackberries that had crowded up against the fence were gone. The tall summer grass with all the secret tunnels and paths we kids had made, gone too. All of it was burnt black, flat to the ground and there was water all over the sidewalk even though it hadn't rained. Daddy was there, with some more policemen. All our neighbors were out in the street and the fire engine was going back up the hill.

Mama carried me and she walked all through the field, back and forth and back and forth. Little puffs of smoke swirled around her shoes as they crunched the stubble of burnt grass. I could see she was upset, so I tried not to cry.

I loved that vacant lot, and the bright sunny days we played there and the fat juicy sweet blackberries on the bramble-bushes that grew through the chicken-wire fence. All summer long, me and Tommy and Jasper and Becky Jones picked berries right off the fence and ate them. They were so good, sour and sweet, dusty and hot from the sun, and they made our lips and our fingers purple.

There was a hole in the fence, way in the back of the lot where we always sneaked in to play. Nobody grown up ever went there. The dry grass was taller than we were and we had made secret trails like tunnels through it, just big enough for us. We pretended it was the jungle and at any minute a tiger might jump out. Now it was all gone.

Mama was carrying me and walking all around the field, where it used to be. The sharp sour smell of burnt grass stung my nose. There was nothing left, just a few tiny flames that made little crackling sounds on the last stems of burning blackberry brambles.

I had seen Jasper's daddy burn off crop stubble in the winter to clear his cornfield for the next year's planting, but it was summer, and this was not a crop field. It wasn't anything; it was just where we played. It was *our field*.

I asked Mama "Why did they burn the field?"

She didn't answer, she just kept on walking and looking at the ground and into the piles of burnt bramble-bushes in all the corners of the field. I started to fuss and cry, but it was too late anyway, my favorite place to play was gone. Mama just kept walking back and forth across every inch of the burnt-out field, like she was looking for something. But there was nothing there, not anymore. I wondered where Tommy was. It was getting dark.

Tommy was five years old and I was three. We always slept in a long narrow little bed, with him at one end and me at the other and toe-to-toe in the middle. That night when Granny put me to bed, Tommy wasn't there.

I didn't see him until the next day. He was very quiet. I'd never seen him that quiet before. Daddy took both of us to the courthouse with him early in the morning. I was a big serious-looking building made out of gray stones with a whole lot of steps going up to it from the street. Behind the courthouse was the police station, and that was where we went.

Other policemen were there in the Squad Room, and they all had uniforms and badges like Daddy's. They looked at us but they didn't smile. Daddy took me to an office where there was a nice lady who was the secretary. She let me sit in a big chair that you could spin around. Daddy took Tommy somewhere else, and they were gone for a long time.

"Where did Daddy and Tommy go?" I asked politely.

"Your daddy is showing your brother what the jail is like," the nice lady answered.

"Why?"

"Because he's showing him what happens to people

who are bad," she said.

"What happens to them?"

"They have to stay in a small room for a long time, and they can't go out and play."

"Why not?"

"They're being punished because they violated the law."

"Oh." I said. "Did Tommy violet the law?"

The nice secretary didn't say. She smiled, and then she said, "How would you like to play with my typewriter?"

When Daddy and Tommy came back, we went home. Tommy was very quiet and he looked scared. I didn't know what was going on, but I think Tommy was in a lot of trouble, and I think it was something about the fire.

Chapter 3: Mama Hill's House

My parents were young then, barely thirty-something. They dreamed of a better life, a new place and a new start. It was going to be an epic adventure, across a continent. So they took a giant leap of faith, and all of us began the journey to California.

I think I was four when all of a sudden one day Daddy and Mama decided to leave North Carolina and go West, "where there are more opportunities," Daddy said. Mama had a girlfriend from High School who lived in Dallas, so that was going to be the first leg of the journey, half way.

Daddy bought a used car and then he put Mama and Tommy and me on a train to Dallas. He stayed behind to sell the house and quit his job at the police department and then he was going to drive to Texas to join us.

I remember the Pullman train. All day we had to sit still on a hard scratchy seat and be quiet. At night the three of us, Mama and Tommy and me, slept in the upper berth. It had thick velvet curtains around it. It was hot and cramped and all it had was a narrow little window where you could look outside at the darkness.

I could see the shapes of strange long buildings that had tall chimneys with trails of smoke coming out of them and little blue lights blinking on the tops of the smokestacks, slowly passing by. That's all I remember.

When we finally got to Dallas, we stayed with Mama's friend Linda and her husband Ed. After Daddy got things settled in Greensboro, he drove the little two-seater Ford to Texas and got there about three weeks after us. Granny wasn't there yet. Then something happened at Linda's house, I don't know what, and we had to leave there at night in the rain. It was chilly and we were wet in the car. The next thing I remember, we were in a small room in a log-cabin motel. We had doughnuts and water for dinner.

The lady that ran the motel must have felt sorry for us, because the next day she rented us a room in her own house at 1521 North Peak Street. Daddy made me memorize the address in case I ever got lost. The first night there was only one bed, so Tommy and I slept on a wicker love-seat thing. We shivered all night with no covers, just our coats over us. The lady's name was Lillian Hill, and the very next day she got us another bed and a couch. It was one room and a bathroom. I washed the dishes in the sink and set the drainer in the bathtub. We ate soup and sandwiches and sometimes Daddy cooked kidney stew with carrots and onions in a tin pie-pan on top of the little gas heater in the bathroom. It was fun.

The house was on the corner and it had a huge yard to play in, rose bushes all around the front, and in back there was a garden with zinnias of every color, and a little vegetable patch with tomatoes and okra. Mrs. Hill was a sweet old lady and she didn't have any children. She told us to call her Mama Hill, and that's what I always called her.

Mama Hill let me and Tommy come downstairs and visit with her any time we wanted to. One time when I was in her kitchen, I told her about how we kept our food in a Coca-Cola cooler in the bathroom and we ate our dinners off of the ironing board. I didn't know it was supposed to be a secret. When she told Daddy and Mama what I'd said, they thought for sure we were going to get kicked out. But instead Mama Hill gave us the whole rest of the upstairs. Then we had another big room with a kitchen set up at the other end of it, and a small room under the eaves that would be Granny's room later when she came.

In the evenings after dinner we would take the couch cushions and lie on the floor and listen to the radio shows, Jack Benny and Ozzie and Harriet The Shadow Knows with Basil Rathbone. He was called the shadow because he had "the power to cloud men's minds so they could not see him." Mama made banana custard pudding with vanilla wafers on top of it and I fell asleep on the floor with my face snuggled into Daddy's big warm hand because it always smelled like fresh garlic from the cooking. I loved the smell of garlic and my Daddy's hands.

Daddy applied for a job at the Dallas Police Department but he didn't get it. When he came home that day, we could tell he was disappointed and he was mad. He told Mama he didn't want to work for "that kind of a police department." That was all he said. I guess Dallas was different. Maybe he didn't want to be a big-city cop and have to shoot people. Anyway, he wasn't a policeman any more, and he never talked about it again.

Mama got a waitress job in a little coffee shop down the street called the Colette Cafe. Then the war ended and the servicemen came home and got all the jobs, so Daddy did house-painting and carpenter work whenever he could get it. He was a sailor when he met Mama, but after he was done I guess he didn't have to go back to the war because he was a policeman and they needed him here. Mama Hill's house was happy for me, so I didn't know it was not as much fun for Mama and Daddy.

When Granny came to live with us again, I was glad. She sewed quilts and I threaded the needle for her on the sewing machine. Mama and Daddy were busy with grown-up stuff, but Granny always had time for me. If she was cooking, she let me stir the bowl. If she was ironing, she taught me how. She stood me on a kitchen chair to reach the ironing board and she let me iron her pretty flower-printed handkerchiefs. I made each one perfectly flat and smooth and beautiful, then folded it just so. I was very proud of myself.

Spring came and it rained a lot. The tree branches had buds on them but they were still bare-naked with no leaves. One day Mama got it into her head that she wanted to go horseback riding. I think she was homesick for Kentucky where she grew up, and Texas had turned out to be kind of a disappointment.

We waited and waited for Tommy to come home from school. You never knew what he was going to do. It was late afternoon and Mama really wanted to go. So just this once, the three of us got into the car and went without him. Mama knew he would be okay because Granny would be there whenever he got home.

Daddy drove us out of town to a place that rented saddle horses by the hour. They were slow, nothing fancy, but Mama had grown up in Lexington and she loved horses. I guess she needed something to lift her spirits a little bit.

We rented three horses; Mama picked them out. She put me up on one of them all by myself. My horse's name was Joe. He was a very big horse. My legs were too short for the saddle, but Mama stuck my feet under the stirrup straps so I wouldn't fall off. She taught me how to say "giddy up" to make him go, and "whoa" and pull back on the reins to make him stop. I tried it and it worked.

The weather was wet and blustery. We rode around on

muddy trails under dripping branches of bare trees, but I was absolutely swimming in happiness. I fell in love with horses, right then and there, forever.

I rode my horse like an old cowhand wrangler. I shook the reins and shouted "Giddy up!" and Joe walked faster, up and down rutted hillsides and muddy creek-beds. I pulled back on the reins and told him "Whoa!" and he stopped. Once he did a trot that bounced me up and down and made my teeth rattle, but I said "Whoa" quietly and pulled the reins just a little bit to make him walk nicer, and he obeyed me. I was thrilled. *I am a horse-rider!*

Mama praised me for doing such a good job, and Daddy even smiled too, a real grin, because I rode my horse so proud, with no fear. When we finally rode the horses back to the barn, the horse-renter man was smiling too. He said I was very brave. I wasn't sure what that meant, but I knew it was something good. That day I learned: *I am brave, and I can do brave things all by myself.*

Just once, I didn't have to be second-best to Tommy, I got to be somebody. It was a great day for me, I rode a horse! It was the best thing I had ever done in my whole life, a pure joy I would never forget, and I would never get over it.

Most parents would have carried a five-year-old child on their lap, but not Mama. She let me ride my own horse.

Since I was born in the middle of the school year, I wouldn't start school till six and a half, so when I was six Daddy taught me to read a little bit so I wouldn't fall behind. He bought me a Little Golden Book and started teaching me how to sound-out the letters to read it. I did pretty well, and I liked the attention. Pretty soon I started reading everything I could find. Books and magazines, wrappers and labels of things. I nearly drove Daddy crazy asking What does this word mean? How do you say this one? Why is the k silent?

I loved how words could tell stories and make pictures, sometimes even more real than real life. What a great thing! I got excited about new words I learned. I copied them down carefully and saved them in a little notebook. I cherished them; they were mine. I said them out loud to myself and memorized how to spell them and what they meant. I hoarded them the way any child collects sea shells or other precious things.

I read Granny's old poetry books and Winnie the Pooh and a big book called Grimm's Fairy Tales that must have been Mama's when she was a little girl. I read dusty books from the shelf behind Daddy's desk, the plays of William Shakespeare and the short stories of Guy de Maupassant. There was a lot of it I didn't understand, but that made it more mysterious, and I was eager to read some more.

By the time I started first grade I had read William Wadsworth Longfellow's poetry and the Rubáiyát of Omar Khayyám from Lakewood Public Library. Reading was wonderful, so I was excited to start school. But when we read The Adventures of Dick and Jane, I thought, *These are the dumbest stories...*

By third grade I still wasn't interested in the books my classmates read, like Nancy Drew Mysteries and Little Women. I read horse stories and histories of wild mustangs and the American Plains Indians. They were wonderful horsemen; they talked to their horses and never used a saddle. That's what I would have done too.

I loved learning things like that, and I loved books

because I could go anywhere and see anything and do anything with just my mind.

Tommy was the rebel of the family and I was the good kid. It wasn't my choice, but it was the job that was available so I was stuck with it. I wasn't perfect, but I did try to be good, and I was, mostly.

In my family, discipline didn't always make sense, as far as I could tell. The punishment for being bad could mean different things. When my brother and I were little, it was mostly a talking-to or a swat on the bottom. When we got bigger, if the crime was serious, that meant the belt. It seemed like Tommy got away with almost anything, and I didn't get punished much either, because I wasn't very interested in doing the things I wasn't supposed to.

My father was a quiet man. He didn't talk much, and never raised his voice in anger. He told us, "Greeks have a dangerous temper." He said if he ever lost his temper, it would be really awful, and that was why he never did.

My father was not the kind of man who would ever get mad and hurt anyone, but since he was the head of the family, it was his job to do the spankings. He always seemed uncomfortable about it. I usually didn't do anything wrong on purpose, and I can't remember ever getting a whipping for anything I did by myself, it was always something Tommy made me do with him, and then we both got a whipping together, usually a half-dozen sharp licks of the belt.

Every time we got a spanking, Daddy would say, "This hurts me more than it hurts you." Or "I'm doing this for your own good." and then he would say, "You should be glad I'm not like my father," and then always the story:

"When I was a kid, whenever one of us got out of line, Pops would round up all four of us (him and his brothers) and whip the tar out of all of us." Then Daddy would pause, for the emphasis, and then, "If one of us got out of line, all of us got the belt, just to make sure the rest of us didn't think about trying it too."

He hardly ever spoke of his father, but when he did, it was very respectfully.

"He taught us the difference between right and wrong" Daddy said. "He made men out of us." I don't think Tommy and I took the story very seriously at the time.

When I was about seven I stumbled onto a discovery. Going up the stairs I slipped, and my shin came crashing down on the sharp edge of the step. The pain was so terrible I could hardly breathe. I started to cry, but it hurt so much I held my breath and clutched my shin. When I stopped crying, it seemed like the pain was not quite as bad. I caught my breath and started to cry again, and the pain got worse. I stopped again, and that seemed to help. I had a brilliant idea: *Crying makes things hurt more!*

The next time Tommy and I got punished for something, I decided to test my idea. Usually we would holler as much as possible, like we were in terrible suffering, so maybe we might get less whipping. But this time was different – I didn't cry at all. Instead, I held my breath and I kept my body rigid. As the stinging belt licks came, I endured them in silence. After just a couple of whacks, Daddy stopped. He looked surprised. Suddenly it was over. After that, I don't think Daddy ever spanked me again. Ever.

When you're a little kid, your imagination is much bigger than you are, and your faith knows no bounds. Every wonderful new thing you see, you want to DO that, or you want to BE that. I wanted to be a cowboy; I wanted to be a firefighter; I wanted to write books and fly airplanes like Amelia Earhart, but more than anything else in the world, I wanted to be a jockey and ride thoroughbred racehorses very fast in the Kentucky Derby.

One day that summer when the grownups were talking, Daddy's friend Jack asked me what I wanted to be when I grew up. I spoke right up all proud and said, "I want to be a jockey and ride race horses!" Everybody busted out laughing, especially Daddy and Jack, like that was the funniest joke they ever heard. I was surprised and hurt. I didn't understand why they were all laughing at me. Mama saw the look on my face.

"Vickie, honey, you can't be a jockey..."

"Why not?" I demanded, and I forced back angry tears.

"Because that's for boys, honey. You can't be a jockey. You could be a nurse, or a secretary, or maybe a teacher. Wouldn't you like to be a teacher? It's just..." she paused, "Girls can't be jockeys..."

My pride was shattered. *Why are they laughing at me? They don't know, I MIGHT do it. I've still got my whole life.*

It was not the first time I'd been told I couldn't have what I wanted just because I was a girl, and there would be many more to come, but I remember that time the most. I remember my hurt and my anger. *It's not my fault! It's not fair! I didn't get to choose.*

I was mad at life for making me a girl. I believed I should get the same rights as my brother, but everybody laughed at me for that. I could just about hear them thinking it, "Isn't that precious! A jockey! Isn't that cute!"

Everybody except Granny. She understood. She said I was "headstrong" because I didn't give up easy. She thought that was good, and I did too.

The ones who laughed at me were people who loved me. They thought they were helping me learn how to live in the world, but they were not. They were teaching me how to live in their world, but my world would be different, and by the time I was grown, their world would be gone. That was one of many times when people would tell me, "you can't do that, because..." But they were wrong.

When winter came again, it was like Dallas winters always were, gray and drizzly every day, until one morning when I walked outside to go to school, all of a sudden the whole world had changed.

Everything was white, so bright it hurt my eyes. A fine mist of tiny ice-specks was drifting down, freezing as it fell. It wasn't snow, it was freezing rain, and it was as pretty as a fairy tale. I looked up at the blank white sky, and there was another surprise. Above our street in front of Mama Hill's house, there were blackbirds, hundreds of them, all in a row, all along the telephone lines.

They were hanging upside down, bobbling in the wind. They looked like clothespins on a laundry line, and they were swinging back and forth like tiny trapeze artists, with their little feet clenched around the wire. When I first saw them dangling there, they looked so comical I started to laugh. In an instant I realized the poor little things were frozen to death. In the middle of the laugh, I started to cry.

The radio said it was the worst winter in Dallas in forty years. When I saw my brother's new argyle plaid socks in so many colors, I asked Mama, "Do I get some too?"

"Oh no, honey, they're boy's socks," was all she said. The rules said girls had to wear dresses while boys got to wear warm pants and knee socks. It didn't seem fair, and it didn't make any sense to me, but the more I learned about things, the more I knew you have to get used to a lot of stuff that doesn't make sense if you were born a girl.

The cold came all at once that year on the tail of a Blue-Norther that blew in without warning, bringing with it two weeks of sleet and freezing rain. When a Norther hits, the temperature can drop as much as fifteen degrees in an hour, and that was what it did.

Everything that was wet, froze. The grass, the roses, the water pipes, the birdbath, and Mama Hill's goldfish pond. I was astonished. It must have snowed in North Carolina, but back then I was too little to go outside, so I had never seen anything like this.

Everything was sparkling white and icy. The air was so cold it shocked my face and made me catch my breath, and when I breathed in, it hurt my lungs like tiny sharp icicles went in there. And every time I breathed out, it made little white clouds in the air, just for a second, and then they disappeared.

The ground was all white and the sky was white and the tree branches were all shiny and black. Everything looked so strange and pretty. The cold was awful but it was beautiful to see. The rain coated every leaf with a thick crystal shell of hard ice. All along the slippery sidewalk, every bush looked like a glittering chandelier, and their leaves made little tinkling sounds in the wind as if they were made out of glass.

The freezing rain kept coming, adding more layers of ice until the weight of it broke branches off the trees and they came crashing down all around. Whole trees broke apart, one on our block split in two. Branches fell onto the street taking electric lines down with them. Power went out all over the city and schools shut down at noon. Parents came to pick up their kids by car, but nobody knew how to drive on ice, and cars went slipping and sliding sideways all over the streets. Some of them ended up in people's front yards and others crashed into parked cars with a loud WHUMP! For us kids, it was as funny as a circus.

There was no school for three days until the worst of it was over. I had to stay indoors for the rest of that first day, but the next day I got to go outside and play. I was allowed to bundle up in pants and sweaters. Since nobody would notice me, it didn't matter if I looked like a boy.

I ran and slid for miles and miles on the perfectly-iced flat sidewalk in front of Mama Hill's house. I did it again and again and again.

I am SO FAST! I am wonderful! I am a famous ice-racer in some faraway foreign place, like Norway where they have the fjords!

Chapter 4: Beacon and Columbia

We lived at Mama Hill's house for about three years before we got a place of our own. Mama found it, a duplex for rent at the corner of Beacon Street and Columbia Avenue, and we moved in right away. School was starting and I would be in third grade. I had a new house and a new school and everything was great. I went skipping around the house singing songs while Mama and Daddy were unpacking.

Our new place was big and it had a real kitchen. All the rooms were in a row: a living room in the front, then a room for Mama and Daddy, then came the kitchen, then a middle room that was for Tommy and me, with bunk-beds. Tommy got the top. And then Granny's room in the very back and then the back door.

Daddy didn't have a regular job yet, but he was working part-time as a waiter. Mama had a good waitress job at Mr. Joe Yee's Chinese and American Restaurant and the first month's rent was paid. I helped unpack dishes out of the newspapers they were wrapped in when they came from North Carolina. We hadn't unpacked the boxes until now.

Daddy was moving stuff in, putting up curtain rods and light bulbs and fixing things. It was hot summertime, 103° outside and even hotter in the kitchen where Mama was working all morning, cooking a special dinner for us. Then she set up the table with all the wonderful food spread out on it in the middle room where it was a little cooler.

Mama's crispy fried chicken, mashed potatoes and giblet gravy, baby green peas, and a big salad with lots of tomatoes, feta cheese, and Greek olives in it, tall jelly-jar glasses of iced tea, and buttery homemade biscuits and honey. It smelled delicious and I was so happy I couldn't stop singing to myself.

Then we all sat down at the table and bowed our heads as Granny asked the blessing. That was something we didn't usually do, so this was a special occasion. With quiet dignity, Granny softly said a very nice prayer.

As soon as the Amen was said I was bouncing in my chair and clapping my hands. I was so excited about the wonderful dinner. And then, Mama reached across the table and slapped me – *hard*.

"Don't be disrespectful!" she snapped.

I gasped in shock. My face went red and hot. I jumped up from my chair embarrassed and confused. Tommy was laughing and everybody was looking at me. I stood there stunned, and then in my shame I ran for a place to hide myself. I rushed into the bathroom and locked the door.

What happened? What did I do wrong?

I had never been punished like that before. Without any warning, Mama slapped me in front of everybody! All I knew was that I must have done something really bad. A minute ago I was so happy, now I was shocked, confused, and ashamed, hiding in the bathroom.

They tried to get me to come out. First Daddy knocked on the door and said sternly, "Come out of there and sit down and eat."

I didn't answer, and I would not open the door. He rattled the door handle. "Open this door!" he said again, louder this time. "Right this minute!" I was scared.

I moved away from the door and sat down on the hard cool floor and leaned against the wall.

What just happened? What did I do? Why did Mama slap me? In the face. In front of everybody?

Then Mama came to the door. In a quieter voice, she said "Vickie, come on out and eat."

But how could I?

Daddy tried one more time too, but I didn't answer. I held my breath so I wouldn't cry. I sat silent as a stone. Outside the door they were silent too, except for Tommy snickering. Daddy said something I couldn't quite hear and they all went back to eating.

I could hear the tinkling of the ice cubes in the delicious iced tea. My mouth felt dry as dust. I heard some muffled conversation, but nobody was talking much. I could smell the tantalizing fried chicken and hear silverware clinking on the good china plates as they all ate. I sat there on the floor, looking at the claw-foot bathtub and the cracked seams of the faded linoleum floor.

I sat there for a long time. Finally I heard the chairs scrape back from the table as everybody got up and carried the plates into the kitchen. Then there was nothing. They all went into the living room and I was left there in the bathroom by myself.

I felt utterly shamed. My face still stung from the slap. Tears ran down my cheeks and dripped from my chin onto my cotton summer dress. I blew my runny nose on the toilet paper. My hurt turned into anger. *Mama has never slapped Tommy.*

All of the beautiful food had been right there in front of me, all the delicious smells and the steam from it, right under my nose. We had a new house and everything was wonderful, and then in an instant, it was all gone, and I was all alone in the bathroom, too ashamed to even be alive. A new wave of misery swept over me. I buried my face in a stack of towels so nobody could hear me cry.

I sat there on the cool linoleum floor, locked away in the solitary confinement of my own making. There was nothing to do but think. Through tears of rage I swore a solemn oath to the bathroom walls: *I hate this house! I will never be happy here!* I vowed I would refuse to be happy, no matter what.

Time dragged by. As the light from the small bathroom window dimmed, I knew that twilight was coming. I tried to figure out what I had done wrong. Somehow I had been "disrespectful." I decided to look it up in the dictionary as soon as I could. *Whatever it is, I swear I didn't mean to be that.*

It wasn't fair, but there was nothing I could do about it. All the wonderful feast was gone and I didn't get a single bite. My belly growled and ached with emptiness. I felt righteously wronged, and I vowed to stay locked in the bathroom forever. *I'll show them!* I thought, in an eight-year-old martyr's sort of way.

By the time it was almost dark, my face didn't burn from the slap anymore and the salty tears on my cheeks were crusty and dry. I knew I had to let it go. That was hard. Mama had slapped me without any reason that I could figure out. *Tommy does bad things all the time and Mama never slaps him.*

After I wallowed in self-pity for a while, I felt a little bit better and I began to get my practical-self back. I knew I had to accept that this was just another one of those things adults do that don't make any sense.

I got tired of staring at the walls and counting the little

blue squares on the linoleum, so eventually, sheepishly, I came out.

I went straight to my bottom bunk and crawled into it with my dress on. I was hungry, but I didn't dare go into the kitchen. The light was on in there, and I didn't want them to see me. Tommy would laugh at me, I knew it. This must have been great fun for him, seeing his shy little sister, the one who hardly ever does anything bad, get punished. I pulled the covers over my head even though it was a warm night. I wanted to disappear. Even more than that, I wanted to not exist.

After a while Mama came and brought me a glass of milk and some graham crackers. I couldn't say anything. I pulled my tangly hair across my eyes so she couldn't know in the dark if there were tears in there. She dragged a chair over from the table and sat down next to my bed, and while I ate the graham crackers she began to tell me a story. She had never told me stories before. It was a story about her, when she was about ten years old, back in Kentucky. I've forgotten some of it now, but the story went like this:

Somebody, maybe her stepfather or a friend of her mother's, told her she could have a horse of her own, if she could catch one. All she had to do was go out to the paddock and catch one. They must have meant it for a joke, because the paddock was full of yearling colts and fillies, all of them were completely untamed. I guess the grownups thought there was no chance in the world that she could catch one singlehanded. But she didn't know that.

I had loved horses since I was four, my dearest dream was to have a horse of my own someday. As she told the story and it was just Mama and me, there in the dark, I could almost see it happening...

"At first I tried to catch the big ones, the stallion colts" she said, "but they were too smart. They took off and never let me get anywhere close. They just wheeled around on their hind legs and bounded away,

Then I tried to trick them and lure them over to the fence with apples. Every time a good one came close enough, I held out the apple, and then real quick I threw the halter rope over its neck. That didn't bother them at all. They just took the apple and then bolted, dragging me along with them until I had to let go to keep from getting crushed against the fence rails.

I tried and tried. I wanted a horse so much. I was getting so discouraged, and I was dirty from all the times I fell down and got dragged through the dirt and manure of the paddock. After a while I gave up on the big ones and tried to catch one of the younger ones. But they were even wilder, and afraid of me besides. There was a bay mare with them who was gentler; I guess they must have put her there to keep the colts quiet. I tried to catch her. She was a brood mare, so it should have been easy..."

Mama's voice got softer remembering, and I swear I could see it too. Feel the tiredness and discouragement. I hoped she could catch one, hoped so hard, almost like it was me...

"...but the mare wanted nothing to do with me either. I went back to the smaller ones, but it seemed hopeless. All I had was a piece of rope and a halter, and even if I got the rope around one of the horses' necks, it just bolted and dragged me with it. All of them were this year's new foals, less than a year old and wild as weeds. They had no intention to get caught.

I kept on trying all day long till after the sun went

down. It was getting dark and I had to go home. I was so tired and dirty I wanted to cry. I was covered with sweat and dirt and cuts and bruises. My fingers were blistered from the rope, but I still would not give up. Finally after it got full dark, maybe the horses got tired too, or they just got bored with it all. I finally caught the smallest one, a runty little colt, but it was mine, and I got to keep it."

I don't know why she told me that story. She didn't say she was sorry for slapping me, but I think she was. There were only a few times when she had ever talked to me like that, just her and me. I think that time was the closest we ever came to knowing each other.

I didn't keep my vow to hate the house at Beacon and Columbia forever, I came to love it. The years we lived there were the best we ever had as a family. Nobody ever told me what I had done wrong but I learned a hard lesson: *It's dangerous to be too happy, and the punishment is quick and terrible.*

For me, expressive behavior wasn't allowed. Tommy had claimed the spot of attention-getter troublemaker, so my position, whether I liked it or not, was the-good-child. My assignment was to be invisible, be good, and be quiet, and if I stepped out of the shadows for even a second, I would surely pay for it. Inwardly I rebelled against this, but in my world, the cost was too high.

I learned to survive by hiding myself in plain sight, by being always wary and vigilant. I knew that even though the rules could not be understood, they had to be learned urgently, and followed carefully. I was beginning to figure out the code of rules and learn the laws of survival.

It looked like boys could do anything they wanted. They got all the best stuff too. Tommy got a wonderful leathery-smelling baseball glove for Christmas one time, and one year an electric train. I got dolls and plastic toy dishes.

Boys could get cowboy boots, but girls could only have stupid ballet slippers, it was the rules. I was quick and strong, and I could run faster and climb trees better than most of the boys, but girls were not supposed to do those things. Girls were not supposed to do anything that was brave or fun. I kept on asking Why not? But nobody ever said. I think they didn't know either.

The next three years from third to sixth grade were happy anyway. My best friend Vivian and her little sister Dimi's family moved from San Antonio to right up the street and the three of us walked home from school together every day, dawdling along. One time we stopped and sat down on somebody's lawn and braided each other's hair.

Tommy was not as mean to me then, at least not all the time. He built model airplanes out of balsa-wood kits from the Hobby Shop and painted them with sweet-smelling paint called "dope." When the paint was dry, he stuck on the decals: RAF, USAF, Flying Tiger teeth, or swastikas for the Luftwaffe. He knew the names of all the fighter planes.

Daddy got a better waiter job at the Greater Dallas Club. Mama's waitress job at Mr. Joe Yee's restaurant was steady and they liked her there. Everyone in the Yee family, from grandmothers to granddaughters, worked at the restaurant, and they respected Mama for the cheerful hard-worker she was. They welcomed Tommy and me on her shift every Sunday afternoon for dinner, like we were part of their family. At work Mama wore a flower-print handkerchief in the breast pocket of her clean white uniform, folded just-so, spread out like a flower, with one corner pointed down on the outside of the pocket in a pretty way, where she pinned her name tag. "Welcome. My name is Ann."

Another summer came. The days flowed along like a lazy river and carried me with them. There was plenty of time. That was when I first started to look at the world around me, and to notice things beyond the end of my own nose.

Sometimes I climbed up into the little pear tree and sat and thought about things like life and God. I would be wondering what God was, but then I'd notice a perfect green pear I could pick, so I did, and I ate the pear and it was warm from the sun and crunchy and sour and sweet at the same time and the juice ran down my chin and I forgot all about God. I just knew what Granny said - that he's always around and he watches out for me and keeps me safe. Even if I wake up in the middle of the night, he's there and I can just go back to sleep.

I never thought anything would ever change. I was sure I would always be me, and Daddy and Mama would always be them. But something was changing and I didn't know what it was, like there were things they needed to say to each other, but they didn't.

The days were blissfully long and at bedtime it wasn't even dark. I lay in my bed and looked out the window at the twilight sky and thought long thoughts. The roofs and chimneys looked like cardboard cutouts, but the sky above them was so deep. It seemed to go on forever and ever, all the way to where God lives.

In the perfect warm evening, everything was sweet and drowsy. I listened to the twittering birds gradually quieting down for the night, while the sky turned the color of lilacs. Granny said heaven is up there, and that's where we go when we die. I gazed up at it and wondered what it would be like to die and go up there. The sky was so huge, so deep and so peaceful. I felt a sadness that I didn't understand, but it faded into the soft summer night, and the very next thing I knew, it was morning.

Sometimes Tommy took me downtown with him on the streetcar. We tried to sneak into movie theaters from the fire escape in back. One time we got in, but the security guard caught us and said he'd call the police if we ever did that again. Tommy just laughed.

"He's so stupid," Tommy said after we left. "I could get back in if I want to." It wasn't for the movie, it was just to sneak in. He loved to break rules and get away with it.

Afterward he would buy us each a chili dog and an orange drink at the Orange Julius, and maybe we would visit some sporting goods stores and look at guns and Bowie knives. I followed after him, careful to never let him out of my sight, because sometimes he slipped away and left me. Then I had to find my own way through downtown Dallas and figure out how to get home.

Most days I played at Vivian and Dimi's house or else I hung out in Granny's room. One time when Granny was in the kitchen, I rummaged around in her dresser drawer. Underneath her funny old undies and I found a pretty little china-porcelain box. Inside of it, wrapped in tissue paper and tied with a tiny pale blue silk ribbon, there was a lock of light-auburn hair. One perfect curl. It was hidden, so I knew, *This is a special thing that somebody treasures.* I felt a little shiver of guilt, like I'd found a secret.

The pretty little curl was the wrong color to be Mama's or mine. My hair was dishwater blonde by then, and as a toddler I'd had yellow-blond hair. Mama's hair was blonde, not a match to the curl either. Daddy's and Tommy's hair was dark. The lock of hair tied with a silk ribbon was a sort of bronze color. Whose could it be? I wondered if it was Granny's hair when she was young, and immediately my imagination leapt into fantasy-time:

A young southern belle in the canopied bedroom of a grand old Kentucky mansion sits before a dresser mirror in her Scarlet O'Hara corset, brushing her beautiful waist-length light-auburn hair that has been bound up properly and gracefully on the top of her head all day...

Granny's hair was gray now, and I had never seen a picture of her when she was young. I touched the little golden reddish-brown curl, held it in my palm for a second, gazing, wondering, then I carefully put it back into the little porcelain box. I still remember the color of it, like bright-polished copper.

When Tommy got bored and came looking for somebody to torment, it was usually me. One day I was playing with my dolls in Granny's room, Tommy came over to aggravate me. He started snapping my arm with a rubber-band until he got me to holler, and then he laughed and walked away.

In a minute he came back and did it again. Each snap really stung, and it made me madder and madder. When he came back the third time, I don't know what got into me, but that time when he walked away, I tossed a little wicker doll-chair at him. It landed smack in the middle of his back and bounced off.

"Good for you!" Granny cheered. The little chair only weighed a few ounces, it couldn't possibly hurt him one bit, but it was an act of rebellion, and that was a big mistake.

Instantly he turned around with a wicked gleam in his eyes. "Okay, NOW you're gonna get it!" he said, and he charged straight towards me.

I ran for the bathroom, slammed the door barely in time, and locked it. But the bathroom had two doors and I knew he would run to the back door next, so I ran there faster. It was an old house and the door didn't fit the frame anymore, it just closed-to, with a screen door hook instead of a lock. I hooked it, but I knew he could reach through the crack with a pencil and lift the hook, so I put my finger on it to hold it down. But he didn't try the pencil trick, instead he threw his whole weight against the door.

I screamed. My finger was crushed between the hook and the door. When I looked at it, the flesh of my fingertip was scraped back into a bloody crumpled blob at the base of the first bend. The space where that flesh used to be was slick bright red raw meat and dripping blood. When I saw it, I screamed again.

By the time Mama got me to the sink to wash it, I was crying full-out. When the water touched it, I jerked it back screaming, splattering pink watery blood across the wall. The nerves in my fingertip were bare, and the water made it hurt a thousand times worse. Granny tried to put some Vaseline on the open flesh to make it stop bleeding, but I shrieked in pain when it was touched, and even when it wasn't touched it hurt so terrible I was gasping to breathe.

I had to spend the rest of the day on my bed with my hand hanging over the side while slow drips of blood plopped onto a towel on the floor. I didn't cry anymore, it hurt too much. I could barely breathe. The old familiar awful angry feeling in my stomach was back for about the millionth time. *It's not fair! I didn't even hurt him!*

The finger was throbbing. I held my breath trying to make it hurt less but it didn't work. As usual, Tommy said it was an accident, but this time he was actually "punished" sort-of. He had to sit on his bed for an hour. As soon as Mama went back to the kitchen, he snickered at me.

"That'll teach you." he said, in a loud whisper.

And it did. My very first act of rebellion had backfired horribly and I had paid a terrible price. Now he sat there, grinning at me with his smug I-told-you-so grin.

The smiles my brother smiles at me are mean smiles. He smiles a different smile for Mama. For her he always does his "Everybody-cherish-me-because-I'm-so-cute-and-adorable" smile. My brother is the only person I know who can smile and still be mean.

It took a week for thin pink skin with no fingerprint on it to grow back. The scraped-back part dried up and got hard and finally crumbled off. After three weeks, most of the finger came back, but because I had "an open sore" the park counselor said I couldn't go into the swimming pool for the whole rest of the summer.

The lesson was crystal clear: It's better to just let people hurt you, because if you fight back, that gives them an excuse to hurt you a whole lot more. I felt trapped in a world where there was no justice and no defense. It seemed to me like meanness has all the power, and the mean people always win. Granny tried to protect me from Tommy as much as she could, and she always took my side, but Mama and Daddy didn't listen to her, they believed Tommy.

Maybe little sisters always get picked on by their big brothers. It's supposed to be okay because they're boys. But Tommy *loved* bullying me. It was like he was cruel for the pleasure of it. He made sure I always knew I was less than him. He kept calling me a sissy, like that meant something bad, but I knew all it meant was, I was smaller than him and not as strong. I couldn't help that. If I could have been bigger, I would have. But right now, I knew I just had to take it, and wait.

I don't want to be a sissy, but I'm supposed to be, because I'm a girl. Girls are not supposed to ever get mad, or stand up for ourself. We're not supposed to be strong, because it's not ladylike. Just like most of the other good stuff, being strong is only for boys.

That went against the very blood in my veins, my Granny's stubborn Kentucky blood. I was stronger than him in some ways, and smarter for sure. I could run faster than him, or anybody. I didn't want to be a lady; I wanted to be *me*. If I had to hide it forever, then I would. *But I would not give it up.*

Daddy and Granny never did get along, and Mama was forever trying to make peace between the two of them. After a while, Granny went back to North Carolina again. Then sometime later she came back to Texas. Altogether she went back and forth between Texas and North Carolina three times. In between, Daddy's mother, my Greek yaiya, came to stay with us for a visit. She had her own apartment in Washington D.C. and another son, Daddy's brother Nick, lived there too.

Compared to Jessie Vaughn, Yaiya Sophia was a very refined and proper lady. She was small, barely five feet tall, but she was strong enough to raise four sons and run a small restaurant in New Jersey all by herself when her husband, Daddy's father, died at a young age, about 40 I think, and Sophia was only twenty-six. That was the story I heard. The youngest son Pete was four years old then, my father George was five or six, and Vick and Nick were each a year or two older. By the time we moved to Beacon and Columbia, the four brothers were scattered all across the country, from New Jersey to Washington D.C. to Arizona, and then us, in Texas.

Yaiya could speak some English but she talked mostly to Daddy, always in Greek. It was a pretty language but I didn't understand a word of it.

She was very religious. She took Tommy and me to the Greek church a few times. It was a mysterious place, with dark paintings of Saint George killing the dragon and other saints and martyrs with gold halos. The air was hazy from candle smoke, and at the front of the sanctuary there was a big statue of poor Jesus hanging on the cross, with the crown of thorns on his head and little drops of blood painted on his carved wooden face. It looked like he was hurting really bad. It scared me, but it didn't seem to bother Yaiya, so I figured it must be okay.

My Yaiya was a devout Greek-Orthodox Catholic, but she also believed in dreams and signs, and she had psychic powers. She told me about how, when she was a young woman, one night she woke up in the middle of the night and she saw her father standing at the foot of her bed.

"He didn't say anything," she told me. "He stood there long enough for me to know for sure I was awake, and then he disappeared. It wasn't a dream, I saw him." She was living in New Jersey and her father was in Greece. The next morning she told her husband, "my Papou is dead," and she cried. He told her she was crazy, but she wasn't.

It was three weeks before the letter came because there was no airmail then, mail came by boat. The news from the relatives in Greece said that Sophia's father had passed away on that very same night. "He came to say goodbye to me," she said, "and I knew that he was gone."

Many years after that, when Mama was pregnant with Tommy, she and Daddy lived with Yaiya in Washington DC then, and one night Yaiya had a dream about the birth of her grandchild. She woke up to the noise of dogs outside in the street, fighting and snarling. She was very upset and she told her son and daughter-in-law, "This is a sign. The baby will be a boy, and he will look like a wolf," she said. "The baby will have pointed ears and he will look like a wolf." They thought she was just being a superstitious old-country grandmother.

When Tommy was born, sure enough, he did have pointed ears, a little bit, and that was not all. Yaiya told me, "The baby was born with thick black hair on his head and shoulders and all the way down his back." *He did look like a wolf.* I asked Mama if it was true. All she said was, "The hair rubbed off in a week or two." All I know is, if an old Greek woman tells you something, you should believe her.

My brother would grow up to be a handsome man, but he never did look like anyone else in the family. He had arched eyebrows and small deep-set eyes, not brown, but black like olives. He had wide lips and a nose that were not like Daddy's or Mama's, and pointed teeth that made him look wolfish when he smiled. His smile was not like anyone else's either. I figured he must take after the grandfather that neither of us had ever met, or else it was just a mystery.

The streetcar ran past our house down Beacon Street. In the summer I rode it to the Lakewood Public Library, my escape from the heat and from my ordinary world. In the library it was deliciously cool and dim. Anybody could go there and stay all day if you wanted to, so I did. In the back was a kids' section that had a window-seat with a faded red velvet cushion that was my spot. I sat with my back to the window and read for hours. Outside the window, sycamore trees fluttered their leaves and scattered little spots of sunlight and shadows dancing across my pages.

At age ten I believed that horses were the most brave and intelligent creatures on earth. I read horse stories like The Black Stallion, and true books about the history of the wild Mustangs, descended from horses that the Spanish explorers brought here on boats a long time ago, before there were any states, and America was wild. There was a book called King Of The Wind, about The Godolphin Arabian, which was the ancestor of all thoroughbred racehorses. Never before had they been so strong and fast. He was smaller, born into the hardships of the desert, so he had great endurance, like me.

In the evening when the library closed, I checked out some books and took the streetcar back home to the house on Columbia Avenue. Mama and Daddy were there, dinner was on the table, and even my brother, who never tired of tormenting me, didn't seem so bad. The radio was telling the six o'clock news and saying "I like Ike" and I guess people did, because he got voted to be the new president.

At ten I was skinny and long-legged. I loved to run, imagining how it would feel to be a glorious and sleek thoroughbred. I tossed my mouse-brown hair like a horse's mane. Mama said I was gawky. It was true I was mostly arms and legs like a yearling colt, awkward standing still, but when I ran I was magically transformed. I was graceful and strong. I was Man o' War, the greatest racehorse that ever lived. Or I was Seabiscuit, the first darkhorse, who came from anonymity into greatness and lifted the spirits of a whole nation.

When I run, my heart flies out over the ground as easily as a bird, and my body simply follows. No one else knows, but in my secret heart, I think it's my destiny to someday do wonderful things.

The time at Beacon and Columbia was the best we'd had since we left North Carolina. Daddy and Mama were both working regular and Tommy wasn't always so mean to me. We did things, all of us together. Daddy traded in the little Ford for a big green 4-door Desoto with a back seat. Sometimes on Sundays we all climbed in and Daddy drove us out into the country. Tommy and I counted spotted cows and shouted out the rhymes on the Burma-Shave signs.

Sometimes we went to White Rock Lake and brought a picnic lunch Mama made. We swam all day in the lake and then Daddy drove us home. The old Desoto swayed and rumbled along so pleasantly with Tommy and me, tired and sunburned in the back seat. The car radio played *I-rene good night... I-rene good night...Good night Irene, good night Irene, I'll see you in my dreams."* I was damp and itchy with sand in the bottom of my bathing suit, but even before the orange sun was all the way down, I fell asleep.

My best friends Vivian and Dimi lived a few blocks away from us then, at the corner of Beacon and Tremont. Summer days we played together and sometimes I spent the night at their house. The three of us girls spent many groggy summer nights on that creaky old Murphy bed. In the hot steamy darkness, the humidity was thick as mud. It lay upon us heavy as a blanket and the heat drugged us into sleep. All through the night we would be waked up again and again by the noise of the streetcars straining at the sharp turn at the corner of Tremont, the shriek and squeal of wheels on track, steel against steel. We would wake up and groan and turn over to allow the hottest part of our bodies more air, even the sweltering air of the summer night in Dallas.

We were leggy, lighthearted, flat-chested and innocent, not even remotely aware of what our lives would someday be. The present was good enough, the future stretched out in front of us, and absolutely everything was possible.

Chapter 5: East Side Avenue, Part One

All of a sudden one day we got the news. Somebody had bought the duplex and now we would have to move out, Just like that. I didn't want to but I couldn't stop it.

Moving wasn't fun this time. I didn't want to leave my back yard and my fig tree. I didn't want to leave Randall Park and my favorite climbing trees. I would miss browsing comic books at the drugstore on the corner, miss my best friends Vivian and Dimi, and most of all I would miss the feeling of being settled and safe and happy.

The new place was much smaller, plain and ugly. It was a square gray box with two apartments, one upstairs and one down. Daddy lived downstairs, and Mama and Tommy and Granny and I lived upstairs.

Mama said she and Daddy were "separated." She tried to talk to me about it once, and she told me, "When people get married, they're supposed to hug and kiss each other in ways they're not supposed to do if they're not married." She said Daddy wasn't doing like he should as a husband. I had no idea what that meant.

In fact I didn't know what any of this stuff meant, but I knew not to question anything grownups did. They were the rule-makers, and I tried to follow the rules, including ones I didn't understand, which was most of them. My brother did just the opposite; he liked to break rules to see how much he could get away with. I don't think he liked it there either, because he started picking on me more.

The house on East Side Avenue sat way at the very back of a large lot, right up against the alley. Instead of a front yard, it had a concrete foundation for a big house, all laid out with sections where the rooms were going to be. There was even a little front sidewalk from the street and three stair-steps to where the front door of the house would have been, but it wasn't, because the house never got built. The people who poured the concrete foundation had also built this little cracker-box house at the back of the lot so they could live in it while they were building the real house in front, but Daddy said city building codes didn't allow more than one residence on a property, so they would've had to tear down the little house before they could build the big house. So they gave up the whole idea and went someplace else and just rented the little house to people like us.

It was plain and drab on the outside, but the inside was interesting. They must have built it out of whatever scrap linoleum and wallpapers they could get cheap. The kitchen wallpaper had huge pink roses on it like should have been in a bedroom. The wallpaper in Granny's room was wide maroon and white stripes with a silver acanthus-leaf border, like in the foyer of a mansion in a movie. Mama's room had yellow and green bamboo, where I slept too until Granny left again, then I got to have her room. I don't remember Tommy's room; I stayed away from him as much as possible.

The downstairs where Daddy lived was smaller and darker. The front room was knotty pine and the floor was concrete with black linoleum tiles. The TV was down there, and the phone. It was always cool and dark, even in the daytime. That was pleasant in the blistering summer heat, but in the winter it was clammy and cold. There was one small window that was always unlocked, that was how Tommy and I went in and out when Daddy was gone.

Daddy's bathroom was a closet with a toilet and a sink, but there was a shower-stall in the kitchen, along with a noisy old refrigerator, a stove, two rusty chrome-dinette chairs and a dinette table with cigarette burns at the edges of its stained pearl-formica top. Daddy's bedroom had just enough space for the bed, one wooden chair, a tall chest of drawers, and a small closet.

The new place felt strange and sad. Mama and Daddy were different too. By that time, Daddy was the head waiter at the Country Club. He was home in the afternoons and he let me hang around downstairs if I wanted to. I sat at his desk and drew pictures of horses while he was in the kitchen with books and papers spread out all over the dinette table, studying a correspondence-course. He didn't mind if I looked over his shoulder. It was boring though, mostly words and no pictures. There were pages of diagrams with squiggly lines, circles and boxes, labeled with letters and numbers.

"What are those things?" I asked him.
"Circus." he said.
"Where? I don't see any circus."
"No," he said, "circuits." He was studying about how to do electronics repair.

I didn't know what was going on with Daddy and Mama but I knew something was. I could feel it, like something you can't see but you still know it's there, and it scares you even though you don't know why. They didn't fight, and there was no big thing that you could see. Daddy finally had a steady job working at the Country Club, but we still never had enough money. He never had talked as much as most people, but now he seemed quieter than before.

In the movies when families fall apart, this is where the father gets angry at everything, gets really mean, drinks too much, and beats his wife and kids. Our next-door neighbor did that, but Daddy didn't. He just got more quiet, sort of going inside of himself. He was there, but sort of not-there, and it was Mama who began to drink.

Mama and Daddy were both gone to work at night, so Tommy and I could do whatever we wanted. Or anyway, whatever *he* wanted.

It was October and it was a dark night with no moon, and the yellow streetlights just made everything more shadowy and scary. He was making me go with him someplace and I didn't know where, as usual. It had been hot all day, so I was wearing a cotton T-shirt and shorts. Now the night was chilly and I wanted to go home.

"Where are we going?" I asked him even though I knew he wouldn't tell me.

"You'll find out when we get there," he said from up ahead of me. I had to hurry to keep up. This was a strange neighborhood I'd never seen before, with a wide street and perfect lawns and really nice houses. It was a long way from East Side Avenue.

"How much further is it?"

He didn't answer.

He took a sudden sharp turn from the sidewalk and I followed after him up a driveway into the deep shadows where the street lights couldn't reach. We went around to the back of the house to where there was a little tool-shed. The door had a big padlock on it. There was one small high window; it was open but it had steel bars across it, about ten inches apart. As soon as I saw that, I knew what he had brought me for.

"This guy has a candy counter in McClintock's grocery

store" he whispered, "and he keeps his stock in here." Then he said, "I'll boost you up."

He wanted me to shimmy through the bars and hand the goods out to him. I started backing up.

"No!" I said, "I can't!" But we both knew he would make me do it.

"Come on," he said, "and be quiet."

I was small for my age, and skinny. Anything I could get my head through, I could get my body through too. He clasped his hands together to make a step, I put my bare foot into it and he boosted me up high enough to reach the window. I poked my head between the bars and then slipped my arms and my chest through.

Inside the shed it was pitch dark and it had a thick oily smell of chocolate. Holding onto one of the bars behind me, I squeezed my hip-bones through and swung my legs to the floor. I was inside.

"Grab some stuff and hand it out," he said in a sharp whisper. He had brought a big grocery bag to put the loot in. Inside the shed I groped around. My fingers found boxes of candy bars, but I couldn't see a thing so I didn't know what kind they were. I grabbed a whole bunch of them with both hands and lifted them up through the bars to Tommy standing outside the window. I heard the paper bag rustle as the candy bars went into it. I could feel my heart beating really fast.

"Good," he said. "Get some more. Hurry up." I wasn't really scared, but I had that same knot in my stomach that I always got when he talked me into something I knew we shouldn't do.

Somewhere far off in the night a dog barked. Except for

that, everything was eerie quiet. I handed out another big handful from another box of some kind of candy, and again I heard the rattle of the paper bag.

"Wait!" he said. "Somebody's coming!"

A streak of fear ran up my back like fingers dipped in ice water. I squatted down and moved to the window-wall of the shed, hoping maybe whoever it was might just look in through the window and sweep a flashlight around, but not unlock the door. They wouldn't see me.

I forced myself to barely breathe so I wouldn't make any sound. I could hear the faint rustling of the tree leaves above the shed, and the smallest sounds of the night.

Then– the crunch of footsteps in the gravel driveway, coming closer. Beside the driveway right next to the shed there was a patch of soft lawn, where the sound of the footsteps stopped. Terror clutched my chest like a fist. I held my breath. My heart was beating so hard I could feel it banging against my ribs.

I waited.

A sharp WHACK! loud as a gunshot. *It was the padlock.*

I crouched in the pitch-black space, shaking, hugging the wall. *It banged against the door hasp again,* louder, rattled a few more times, and then there was silence.

I waited. It seemed like a long time. Then I waited some more, just in case. Then I stood up, slowly and carefully, and looked out the window. There was nothing.

I started to climb back through the bars. It was harder this time because there was nobody to boost me up. My hip-bones got stuck halfway, so I had to kick and grunt to push myself through. I got my legs free and managed to drop to the ground, more or less head-first, and still land on my hands and knees. I scrambled to my feet with a loud shower of loose gravel, and darted out the back way through the alley to another street.

Tommy was nowhere to be found. The street sign said Montgomery Court. I didn't know where that was, but he had left me in strange places lots of times, and I always found my way home. This time it took a while. When I got home, the house was all dark. Tommy wasn't there. I went to bed.

In the morning, Tommy gave me three Mr. Goodbars and he said "Next time we'll get more."

I didn't say anything, I just thought it to myself. *Nuh-uh, there's not gonna be any next time.*

When winter came again it was cold and rainy every day. All the trees in the yard went bare-naked of leaves and looked sad. The winter dragged on and on and the house was always shivery, so I took a lot of hot showers and stayed near the gas heater. It took forever for Spring to come, but when it finally did, I told myself *Okay, now everything will get better.*

But it didn't. Mama told Tommy and me that she and Daddy might get a divorce, but they were staying together for us kids' sake. That made me feel guilty. Maybe if Tommy and I were not there, they could have been happy. I felt ashamed, and helpless.

If it wasn't for Tommy and me, maybe Mama could be happy now. She wouldn't have to work so hard to take care of us and feed us and buy us shoes and everything.

I feel awful about it, but what can I do? I didn't ask to

be born, it just happened, and I couldn't help it.

I wanted to tell her, *This isn't happy for us either.* But I didn't say anything.

Tommy was getting meaner. Any time he could make me holler or run from him, he did. He loved to make me shriek with pain or fear. I think he enjoyed my fear the most, because it was like making a puppet dance. It was even better than a puppet, because I was alive. Something he could control that was alive.

By then Tommy was almost fourteen and in Junior High, and he had his own thing going. He walked with a swagger and wore his jeans way down on his hips, and he had a perfect "ducktail" haircut like James Dean. He was running with some other teenage punks and getting in trouble at school. He had already failed in grade school and got put back a year, now he got put back again. He wasn't dumb, in fact he was very smart. He just wasn't interested in school. He was a rebel and that was what he wanted to be. He wanted to stand out, he had to be special. Even when they made him go to summer school, he didn't care, he just didn't go. Mama couldn't make him. I guess she just tried not to think about it.

When we first moved to East Side, Mama got a new job working nights at the Diamond Horseshoe bar and grill, so I didn't see her much after that. She was asleep when I left in the morning, and already gone to work when I came home from school. Granny made supper for Tommy and me, biscuits and gravy and boiled chicken wings with collard greens. But after a while Granny went back to North Carolina again, and then I came home from school to an empty house. But there was bread and peanut butter in the cupboard, and every morning Mama left two little stacks of quarters on the kitchen table, lunch money for Tommy and me so we got a hot meal at school.

In the evenings I went downstairs to Daddy's apartment and watched Ozzie and Harriet on the black and white TV set. Harriet was the Mom, and she was always baking cookies. Their family had two kids too, Dave and Ricky. I had a crush on Ricky. They all sat down at a table to eat dinner every day, all of them together. I wondered where they lived. They sure didn't live on East Side.

It was lonely. We were not the same family anymore. After we left Beacon and Columbia, we were not really a family at all, but I didn't know that was not the way other people lived, except on TV. We didn't do things, all of us together anymore. Daddy and Mama didn't see each other or talk to each other much, and when they did, they didn't smile. Something was wrong. I had heard about divorce from country songs, but all I knew was, it always made everybody unhappy.

All of it was confusing. I didn't know what was going to happen. I felt sort of scared in the pit of my stomach and I didn't know why. My friend Kathy at school told me "It means your Daddy is going to go away, and you won't see him anymore."

Tommy and I had both learned how to manage on our own. He was running around with some kind of gang, and I played at my friend Patricia's house most of the time. Her grandmother wouldn't let Pat come to my house anymore after Tommy accidentally shot her in the eye with his BB gun.

Patricia lived two blocks down the street with her little brother Mike, her granny Ruth, and her mother Maxine. Both of the women were nurses in the Emergency Room at

Parkland, the big County Hospital of Dallas. They were always kind to me. They took me along with Pat and Mike to the movies or the lake, and lots of times they fed me. They didn't know much about my family except that there was nobody home where I lived, and no lunch there.

I was free to go to Pat's house whenever Tommy was gone, but when he was home, I was trapped. I had to pass the doorway of his room to get to the stairs, and he could easily catch me in the hall and keep me prisoner. So instead, very quietly, I climbed out the window.

My room was on the second floor. I carefully went out backwards on my belly, feet-first, held onto the windowsill and slid my toes down the outside of the house until I could feel the narrow wooden ledge at the seam where the first floor and the second floor came together. I braced my feet there for a minute, then I took a deep breath, pushed off, and dropped to the ground. It stung my feet, but even if Tommy heard me and came running out, I could dash down the alley and he could never catch me.

Then I could play at Patricia's house, or maybe we'd go to the park, or go looking for good roofs to climb. We got up onto people's roofs from their fences or garage roofs or maybe a telephone pole. I loved being up high. With our bare toes securely gripping the grit-surface of the roofing, we scampered around as happy and fearless as squirrels.

We liked to roam the run-down parts of Dallas where there were old Victorian houses with turret towers and gabled roofs like the mansions in Dracula movies. They were crumbling and ready to fall down, and boarded up, but we would find a spider-webby broken window where we could get in. Then we would creep all through the empty house, peering into spooky rooms and dark musty-smelling hallways where every footstep, every whisper, echoed loud and strange.

We wandered overgrown gardens of tangled rosebushes and thick jasmine vines pulling down their trellises. We discovered secret mossy-green fish-ponds with broken angel statues. All the abandoned places belonged to us. We were explorers like Lewis and Clark, and whatever we found, we claimed it as our own.

Patricia was eleven and I was twelve, but she was more daring than I was. My granny would've called her "bold as brass" and would not have approved of her. Pat taught me how to snitch things from the dime-store. Little toys, natural-pink lipstick, nail polish, and those tiny bottles of cheap perfume. There was a certain thrill to it, and we were both old enough to know better. Then we got caught.

A strange man, the owner I guess, took us to the back of the store to a dark gloomy storage room and told us very seriously, "I'm going to have to tell your parents."

We begged and pleaded. "Please don't tell them! Please! We'll never do it again, honest." We knew we would both get a whipping for sure. Then he said if we took our panties off and let him touch us down there, he wouldn't tell on us.

"No, I can't..." I said, and I looked around for a place to run. "Mama told me not to do that." Pat didn't look scared at all. She looked like maybe she was thinking about it.

"Come on!" I said. I grabbed her arm and yanked her with me and we both ran past him, back out into the store as fast as we could, through the store and out to the street. We never looked back and we never stopped running till we got all the way to her grandmother's house.

On Sundays Patricia and I would scrub our faces, comb our hair neatly and pin it back with bobby pins, get dressed up as nice as we could, and go to church. A different church every week. Baptist, Presbyterian, Methodist, I think every denomination except Catholic. We were a little bit afraid of the Catholic, because it was all so sacred and holy, and the nuns were kind of scary. They had those black capes on their heads and they didn't have any hair. They wore black dresses no matter how hot it was, and their long black skirts reached all the way to the toes of their lace-up old-lady shoes. And they had those big crosses with poor Jesus suffering on them that hung down the front of their blouse.

But the Methodist and Presbyterian, Church of Christ, and Baptist were not scary at all. The church ladies wore pretty hats and little white gloves and flowered silk dresses, and they smelled really nice. They would say to each other, "Isn't that adorable? Two sweet little girls, all on their own, coming to church?" We were always welcomed wherever we went. We were *adorable*.

Our favorite churches were, hands-down, the Baptist. They had the happiest hymns and everybody sang them real loud. We got to know the words, like "Rock of ages cliffed for me" and "Are you washed in the blood of the Lamb?" My favorite one was "Leaning on the everlasting arms." They all had a good rhythm and the words were easy.

One Sunday there was a Baptism. The blessed person had to walk with the preacher right into a huge glass fish-tank full of water behind the altar, up high where everybody could see. They waded out together and then saying a set of special words, the preacher dunked the person's head under the water! In their Sunday clothes and everything! All the people shouted Praise-the-Lord! and Thank-you-Jesus! and it was a wonderful show.

The blessed person almost got drowned, but then they popped back up again sputtering, with their hair plastered down like a wet cat. But they had received the Holy Ghost, and the whole congregation shouted out, *Hallelujah!* and we did too.

Right after I turned twelve, Mama took me aside to give me The Talking-To. In Texas, boys got the talking-to about sex, and girls got the talking-to about "being a lady." She sat down next to me on the bed and she said, in her most serious voice,

"Vickie Honey, You're gonna have to stop running through the neighborhood, jumping over the hedges and all that. It's time for you to start acting like a young lady."

I remember that day, clear as glass. That was the day she told me that all the things I liked best, "nice girls don't do that." She said I had to give up climbing trees (she didn't know about the roofs) and stop galloping through all the vacant lots, parks, and people's yards, leaping over the fences and hedges like a steeplechase racehorse. I would have to stop running.

How could I stop running? Running was the thing I loved! I could run faster than anybody, faster than Tommy so he couldn't hurt me. Running made me feel good, feel special. Whenever I ran, I felt so strong and free.

Shocked with despair, I thought, *Act like a lady? What does that even mean?* But I understood one thing clear enough: *it's not okay to be me* anymore. It was time to "act like" something else, and that meant I was supposed to give up everything I was good at, including the one thing that made me really happy. I was not allowed to run any more.

It was the same old rule again. Just because I was born a girl, I was supposed to give up the things I loved. I was supposed to "behave like a young lady," but I had no clue how to do that, and I didn't even want to know.

But I tried. I said I would, and I did. I learned how to hide who I really was, and I tried my earnest best to be whatever everyone else expected me to be. Tommy had taught me to be a victim, and now Mama taught me to be a martyr. That was my inheritance.

It's not fair! Why do I have to give up the things where I'm strong, the things I'm proud of about myself?

Or else hide them forever. Okay then, I would hide. And maybe I would lie and pretend, but I would not give up. Rebellion was in the Kentucky blood of my unconquerable Granny Vaughn, and her blood was in me too.

East Side Avenue was lonelier than the old place and it didn't have a grapevine or a fig tree, but every spring it had an overgrown wild garden of flowers that somebody must have planted a long time ago in some of the empty compartments of the concrete foundation, and year after year the flowers came back

There were tall blue Columbines sticking up from the grass and bright yellow brown-eyed Susans barely peeping out. Best of all were the poppies. A great waving ocean of colors, with silky fluttery scarlet petals and purple centers, like a swaying carpet of red and green. All day the hot wind pushed at them, but they rose up again and again. They were like brave soldiers, not for war, but just for being beautiful, and nothing could stop them.

There's something elegant and glorious about poppies,

and they have a wild weedy smell that's not like anything else in the world. All summer my poppies danced in the sun and wind. My garden was like a place in a fairy tale, and all of it was mine.

Sometimes at night I sat on the cool concrete steps at the front of the foundation-house all by myself, and looked up at the dark sky. There weren't many stars, not like in Greensboro where the stars came out every night, milky-white with little halos around each one like they were melting into the sky. I felt lonely and I didn't know why.

That summer, Daddy set out all by himself in the car for a three-week trip to see his brother Pete in Arizona. I think he needed somebody to talk to. Uncle Pete already had a divorce, so maybe he could help Daddy understand what was happening to him, and to us. Daddy drove the old DeSoto through the huge empty deserts of Texas, New Mexico, and Arizona. I guess it gave him a lot of time to think, and when he came back, he was different.

I didn't know when it had started, the space between Mama and Daddy, but gradually it grew. I think she felt it, but there was nothing she could do to stop it. It was like the sea-tide that comes with the cycles of the moon.

She never said anything mean about him. That was not the way she was. I know she loved him but she never knew how to ask for what she needed for herself. I guess he didn't give her what she needed, and so the need grew, and she started to become that to him. Needy. He was not strong enough for that, and I think it must have made him feel like a failure.

Men need to feel like heroes. The more Mama needed him and the more he failed her, the more he pulled away inside himself, where no one could reach him.

Coming to Texas was a breaking-off point between two different lives. All of us moved from a small town to a big town. Daddy went from a proud job to no job. Maybe leaving the police department was harder for him than any of us knew. He kept his badge for the rest of his life in a small wooden box of his personal treasures, and when he died, it was given to me.

Chapter 6: My Granny Vaughn

Jessie Vaughn was a remarkable woman for her time, or any time. She was strong, independent, self-possessed and dominant in both of her marriages. Some would say a domineering woman. She was a realist, practical and unsentimental. With what little I know about her, it seems like she was someone who never settled for less than full ownership of her life.

In her younger days he was called headstrong, stubborn, willful, and other things that a proper Kentucky lady should not be. But when I knew her, she was Granny. Old and slow and nearly crippled, but she still stood her ground. She had the soul of a warrior. She went her way quietly and she didn't say much, but everybody knew she was a force to be reckoned with.

For me, Granny was a large soft sheltering place. She was 65 when I was born, and had suffered a stroke that made her deaf and disabled. By the time I was two years old, she had recovered enough to "get around," and she became my refuge and my fortress. Tommy could manipulate Mama, and through her he could get some control over Daddy. Me, he could terrorize freely. But not Granny. She would not be manipulated, fooled, or intimidated by anyone. She feared nothing, except being put into the County Home, which was the place old folks got put by their grown children when they got too weak to fight anymore.

Daddy called her "a mean disagreeable old woman," but for me she was always gentle and kind. He called her "headstrong," but that sounded like a good thing to me. In her old age she was still an iron spirit, but for me she was the soul of infinite patience. Whatever she had been before, whatever the sins of her past, she loved me. It was Granny and me, partners. If nobody else had the time for us, it was still okay; we had each other.

She always had time for me. She listened to my endless baby chatter and said, "Do tell!" and "My, my!" and I knew she was deaf, but that was okay, because she always knew what I meant.

Whenever Daddy got mad at her, he called her "a bossy, old woman" and other things which she pretended not to hear. She had a hearing aid but she hated the thing and refused to wear it. She claimed to be "deaf as a post," but I was not so sure. Anyway, she never said anything about him, and I think that drove him crazier than anything she could have said.

Daddy said Jessie Vaughn had four husbands. "She either divorced 'em, or just "ran 'em off," he said. "She even shot one of them, and claimed it was in self-defense." I don't know if that was true or not. It could have been. But anyway, nobody died.

Granny wasn't awfully fond of her son-in-law either. Maybe she disapproved of him because he was out of work so much. Well, to be fair, when we came to Texas, the war ended and all the soldiers came home and got all the jobs.

"You don't want to spend your best years on a man that can't carry his own weight," Granny told her daughter, "You'd just as well get shed of him and go on about your business." Jessie Vaughn was not shy to speak her mind, but whether it was good advice or not, we'll never know, because Mama didn't take it.

Sometimes if Daddy got upset with me for something, he would say to Mama, "She gets that from her Granny

Vaughn. She's got that hardheaded-streak, just like Jessie Vaughn." He said that every time I tried to stand up for myself (which did me no good anyhow). There may have been a grain of truth to it, but I said, *NO, I'm not just like Granny Vaughn.* Because from the very start, I knew, *I'm not just-like anybody.* I was always and only just like me.

Tommy loved to torment Granny almost as much as he loved to torment me. He would hide her teeth or her glasses or one of her shoes and then laugh while she searched for them. She knew he had done it. "He does these things just to vex me," she said. But Mama said "You must have misplaced them." She didn't believe Granny and she didn't believe me. She suspected we were in cahoots against Tommy. Well, maybe we were.

When I was little, Granny was my sidekick, my partner and my protector from all the hurtful and scary things in my world. I could run to her and hide behind her skirt when Tommy was chasing me. She would put one arm out and catch him with the palm of her hand on the top of his head and hold him at arm's length so he couldn't hurt me. He kept right on charging, swinging his little fists wildly, trying to punch her in the stomach and kick her poor arthur-itus knees, but he couldn't reach her because her arm was longer than his arms and legs were. He looked like he was doing a silly little dance, flailing his arms like a windmill. Then he would stomp off, calling her names. She told him, "Your sister is not your personal punching bag." I didn't know what a punching bag was, but I knew I was safe when she was around. Mama got upset with her when Tommy went and told her that Granny had pulled his hair. She never did, but I think she would have, if necessary, to protect me. Mama always believed him, no matter what. Again and again I wondered, *Why can't she see?*

After I got bigger I played in Granny's room with my dolls and my books. I threaded the needle of her old Singer sewing machine and changed the bobbins for her, while she made quilts or sewed doll clothes for me. The sewing machine ran by a foot-treadle, a flat ironwork plate at the bottom of it near the floor. When Granny rocked that foot-treadle back and forth with her feet, the machine went humming along and the needle went up and down, stitching seams and making nice little whirring and clicking sounds.

I turned the radio on and sang old-fashioned love-songs on the FM station, about lost loves and broken hearts. I knew all the words and sang to myself. Sometimes Granny gave me scraps of bright colors and I would fashion garments for my dolls, anchoring them with my own needle and thread and a tiny silver thimble. She kept them in a small drawer of the sewing machine's wooden cabinet just for me. Any sort of thing I made, whether it was a doll dress or a drawing or a little poem, Granny praised me to the very skies for it.

The stroke must have taken some of the starch out of her sails. She was slow and shuffling, but that was just the right speed for me to keep up with. And neither age nor illness ever took the stubborn strength out of her character. Daddy called his mother-in-law "the most cantankerous woman on earth" and he said she had "a will of iron, the determination of Job, and the combustible temper of kerosene." But she never was anything but gentle to me. I loved my Granny more than anything. She was the safe harbor from which I could venture out on my tricycle unafraid, and know she would be there every time I came back up the hill.

I never knew much about Granny's early life or about my maternal grandfather, except that they had lived in

Lexington Kentucky where the famous Kentucky Derby race was run every year. As a child I had fantasized that my grandmother Jessie was an aristocrat, a southern belle, beautiful and proud like Scarlett O'Hara. I imagined her with long wavy hair that reached all the way down to her waist when it wasn't pinned up high on her head in that elegant way all the women wore their hair back then. It was gray now, but she still wore it up like that.

In my imagination, she was one of those society ladies at the racetrack, wearing a fancy hat, drinking mint juleps. There would be pure-blooded racehorses, and lean young jockeys in bright-colored racing silks, and everything was elegant and wonderful. Well, for all I knew, it *could be* true.

Mama never told me about her mother or her childhood until one of the last letters she wrote to me before she died. That was the first time I learned what it was like for her, to be Jessie Vaughn's child. She wrote:

"Dearest Vickie,

In your letter you asked about your grandmother Jessie Vaughn, what her life and mine was like long ago. I will tell you as much as I know about your ancestors, from scraps of information my mother told me about her life.

Her father's name was George Blakeman and her mother's name was Amanda. They lived on a large farm inherited from his father. They were not well-off but lived comfortably, farming the land with the help of several Negro families living on their land. The slaves had been freed, but with no education or money, many chose to stay on with white families that had been good to them even when they were enslaved. Kentucky was neutral during the Civil War and sympathetic towards runaway slaves, and often helped them on their way to the north. George and Amanda Blakeman had four children: Robert the eldest, Belle who died when she was 16, the younger son Ben, and then 14 years later, Jessie, my mother, was born.

When Jessie was very young, her father went blind and her mother had to take over the management of the farm. Money was scarce and the Negroes were given a share of the money earned from the crops, so there was very little cash, but the parents managed to send Robert to college. Before he was able to finish, the Spanish-American war broke out so he joined up. He became a lieutenant and received many decorations. Then there was enough money for the younger son Ben (Benjamin Franklin Blakeman) to go to college. He got a masters degree and taught Latin and Greek at Center College in Danville Kentucky for 20 years. After the Spanish-American war was over, Robert took up his studies again and became a lawyer. In his later years he wrote a book on Kentucky law.

On the farm Jessie, my mother, was growing up. She was raised mostly by an old colored Nanny because her mother was running the farm, keeping the books, and taking care of a blind husband. I think my mother got about the same as a high school education while living on the farm to help with the work, as girls were often home-schooled in those days. When her father died, her two older brothers Robert and Ben were gone from home and making a living on their own.

So then the widow (my mother's mother, your great-grandmother) decided to sell the farm. She signed over enough land and the homes of the Negro families living on the place for them to do quite well on their own. She gave them livestock, cows and mules and farm equipment. Then she bought a house in Lexington for herself and my mother Jessie, where they took in boarders.

Mother began training to be a nurse at Garfield Hospital in Washington DC, but she never did graduate because her mother became ill, so she went back to Lexington to take care of her and the boarding house.

That was when my father, Robert Fletcher Long, came on the scene. He was from Peoria Illinois. He was broke and out of work, but his mother sent a note saying he was a distant relative and if they would put him up for a while, he would repay them. His mother was a third cousin of my mother's mother, so they took him in. He looked for a job, and paid his way with them by doing odd jobs and repairs around the house, like painting, and patching the roof.

He was young and handsome. People said he had a charming personality, and he had blue eyes and curly light auburn hair. Mother hadn't had much opportunity for romance when she was young, and now an old maid of 35, she was swept off her feet by his attentions. He got a job as an auto repair man but stayed on with them. He had lived with them about a year when Jessie's mother died. He then asked my mother to marry him.

He was 11 years younger than her, but he said that didn't matter, that he really loved her. Being a drifter and not too fond of work, he figured that the house and money she had in the bank would be a good thing for him. My mother was 36 when they married. He was my natural father and I was legitimate.

He couldn't hold a job very long, and soon she had

to take up nursing to support them. He worked odd jobs like carpenter at the time of my birth. But he drank so much that she ran him off, got a divorce and sold the home in Lexington, then took me, at two years old, to San Francisco California.

People didn't go to the hospital as much in those days, nurses stayed in their homes and cared for them. Mother found work nursing and said she couldn't keep me with her, so I was boarded with a German woman and her 12-year-old daughter.

The woman who kept me was Mrs. Searle. She was good to me and I loved her and called her Mama Searle. I was just learning to talk, and she and her daughter spoke German to each other so I picked it up. I couldn't speak much English until I was almost 5 years old. Mother said she visited me when she could, but often she would be on cases where the patient had a disease I might catch from Mother if she visited me. Anyhow that's the story I was told later. I only saw her about once a month. Then when I was about three and a half, she decided to go back to Kentucky. I was broken-hearted to be taken away from Mama Searle.

We went by train and had a berth on a sleeping car. Mother said I woke up during the night crying and talking baby-talk in German. She was almost a stranger to me. I had learned mostly German, so English was still a strange language for me. She was a 42-year-old woman with a young child she couldn't understand and no husband or relatives for help.

Back in Lexington Kentucky she took a room in a boarding house and made arrangements for the landlady to take care of me while she looked for work. I was left with strangers again, lonely and scared. But Mother must have had a little money saved and she didn't go out so much on nursing cases for a while. I guess my mother tried to understand me and show me some affection, but she wasn't used to children and became angry and frustrated trying to make me talk English and behave. I remember getting slapped and my hair pulled a lot and being afraid of her. I was glad when she went out, because the old landlady didn't keep close watch over me and I could roam the house and play outside when mother was gone.

Then the landlady's widowed brother came to visit, and he met mother. Next weekend he asked mother out to a movie. So the courtship began. I liked him from the start because he always noticed me. Most grown-ups ignored me like I wasn't there. He brought me candy and patted me on the head and said I was a pretty little girl. No one had ever said that to me! Of course he was mostly trying to get mother to like him. He had been a widower for several years and was living alone except for his 17- year-old son Howard. I don't know how long the courtship lasted, but then they got married.

You asked if your Granny was a southern belle. No not really, she was more like what in those days was considered "a handsome woman." Dark brown hair and hazel eyes. Rather bossy, strong and healthy. Just what Daddy needed to keep house for him and his son. It wasn't exactly a love match, but advantageous for them both. It was a home for me and her. She wouldn't have to go out to work and leave me with someone. I guess it was an ideal arrangement, it was for me at least. I adored my stepfather, and always called him Daddy, I had never known my real father. He had a library of books, and there was the Kentucky River just beyond our front door, horses to ride, and 14 acres of beautiful country to play on. We had chickens, cows, pigs and kittens. Things I'd never seen before. This lasted eight years, the happiest years of my childhood. I was 12 or 13 when she left him and nearly broke my heart. From there she took me to Greensboro North Carolina.

I guess I'd better stop here or I'll never get this mailed to you. Later I'll tell you about the events that occurred from then on till I met your father and we got married, and about the time there was a fire in the vacant lot, right next to our house in Greensboro.

–Love, Mama

She did write later about the fire, but I never knew how she and Daddy met.

I think Granny always had a wanderlust, and as she got old she had a longing to go back to Greensboro. She had made the trip twice before, and then came back to Texas. I think she wasn't very happy living with us, even at Beacon and Columbia. Then when we moved to East Side Avenue and things got worse between Daddy and Mama, she must have known, even though Mama tried to hide it from us kids.

Granny had lived a hardworking life, and now she was in constant pain from her arthritis. She couldn't manage the stairs anymore, so she could only sit in her room all day and sew, or read with a big magnifying glass. I was in school, so I didn't need her as much as before. Things must have been lonely for her. She wanted to go back to North Carolina to spend her last years with her old friends.

We couldn't afford the train fare, but Daddy finally gave in, only on one condition. He told Mama, "If she goes back out there this time, she's not coming back here. She's got to choose one place or the other!"

The night we put Granny on the train was the strangest and saddest time for me. I knew somehow that a part of my life was ending, I could feel it, and I think Mama knew it too. I don't remember much about that night, just the images of the train station, because I have seen it again and again in my dreams.

There are two large heavy wooden doors, side by side. They have thick glass windows through them so you can see inside. Both doors have long shiny brass handles to open them with, that look very serious and important like the handles on a casket.

Inside the station it is noisy and smoky and dim, full of people walking around in a hurry and talking and carrying bags and dragging trunks like Granny's. Negro porters are pushing little carts full of more bags and trunks. A whole lot of people are going someplace on the trains. A scratchy loudspeaker voice overhead calls out the names and numbers of the trains that are coming and going and which track they are on.

We all said goodbye. Granny bent down to kiss me on the cheek, and she patted Tommy gently on the head. Mama and the porter walked with her to the boarding platform while Daddy and Tommy and I waited near the big doors. When Mama came back we all went out to the car and Daddy drove us home.

They didn't talk. It was getting dark. I looked out the car window and my stomach was trembling. I felt sick in a strange way and I didn't know why. I knew Granny was leaving again. She had left before, but it seemed different this time. I didn't know I would never see her again.

With one less mouth to feed, things would be a little bit easier for Mama, but the night we took Granny to the train, she cried. It was the only time I ever saw her cry, but I bet it wasn't the only time she did. She probably always hid someplace to cry, like me.

I remember Granny's tired old eyes; they were kind and watery blue. She listened to me with her eyes, because she couldn't hear. I knew she was deaf, but it didn't matter, because she always listened to me as if I were smart and special. I never knew it then, but she loved me in ways that she had not been able to love her own child. She was old when I was born. Maybe living so long had changed her. For me she was always the same, completely patient and kind.

The very best thing about my Granny was that she was always there, never very far away. When I was small she was my rock, my mooring place, and my shelter in any storm. In Greensboro, winter evenings before I went to bed, she would call me into the kitchen where it was warm, and have me sit on a little stool at her feet. She put a tiny speck of butter on the top of my head, and as it melted she brushed it all through my baby-fine blonde hair. It made me feel all melty and sleepy. Mama scolded her for that, and told her not to do it, but she did it anyway.

My most treasured memory of my Granny was just the warm comforting softness of her. In my first few years on earth I rested cozy and safe in her lap on the front porch. Her rayon-silk dresses smelled of lilac dusting powder and a whiff of spirits of camphor for her arthritis. I clung to her bosom while she rocked me to sleep in the porch swing or her rocking chair. All my world revolved slowly and calmly around the quiet summer night and the squeak of the swing or the rhythm of the rockers on the creaky boards of the front porch.

Out in the night a thousand crickets sang, and their music traced patterns on the darkness like lace. A big round cookie moon came up and slowly climbed the evening sky, and the little white stars began to peep out, one by one by one, until the dark sky was sprinkled with thousands of them. The whole starry universe flowed over us like a river, and with everything in my world warm and safe, blissfully sweet, and perfectly perfect, I fell asleep.

My grandmother was not a saint. She had never been beautiful or aristocratic the way I imagined. She may not have been a very good mother, and as a mother-in-law she must have been very challenging. Tommy was Mama's and Daddy's favorite, somehow I just wasn't as good. I knew I was just "the other child." But to Granny, I was special. I was her favorite and I knew it. That changed how I felt about myself, and built a bedrock of faith on the inside of me that would hold firm through a lifetime of storms.

Her respect gave me an assurance that I counted for something. She taught me, not with words, but with a steady, quiet love, that no matter what anybody said, *I was good enough.*

Chapter 7: East Side Avenue, Part Two

Through some of the times when Daddy couldn't find any work, Mama supported all of us on her waitress pay and tips. Waitressing didn't pay much but without a high school diploma it was the best job she could get. She was a good waitress too, and she did all she could for us, but when we moved to East Side Avenue, things got harder. A lot of times there was nobody home and there was no food in the house.

So I went to the big Safeway store, strolled around to look casual, and stole something. Twinkies or cupcakes maybe, or a can of chili. Something like a loaf of bread was too big. It had to be something small enough to hide, so I could walk out with it. One time I stole a package of pork chops. It was the strangest feeling, the package of cold meat tucked up under my dress against my belly. But after I got those pork chops home and fried them up with lots of pepper and salt, oh they were *so good*.

My playmate Patricia had a collie dog named Lady. Pat knew how to go through the big swinging doors of the butcher's area in the back of the store to ask for dog bones. They had boxes and bins full of "ends" of the chops and steaks, where it wasn't as nice, or it had too much fat or too much bone. If you asked for dog bones, they would let you take all you wanted. It was perfectly good meat. Pat took some for her dog, and I took some for myself.

If they asked me what kind of dog I had, I would say, "A big dog." If they asked me what my dog's name was. I said "Skipper." I did have a dog once, a stray I named Skipper. He wasn't big, and after a few days he ran off, but anyway there actually was a dog named Skipper once, so it wasn't really a lie. Not completely anyway. Well, okay, it was a lie. I was not afraid to lie and steal. I was a survivor. Ashamed, but not afraid.

Out by the loading dock in back of the store, at the end of the day they set out boxes and baskets of stuff to throw out. All sorts of good food, and they were just throwing it away! If you got there before the truck came, you could get potatoes and turnips and beets and greens, even tomatoes and peaches and freckled bananas that were clean and perfectly good. Well not perfect, but good. Some were bruised or overripe or maybe they had some moldy spots, that's all. For me it was fantastic; I could just help myself to all that food and it wasn't even stealing – it was okay to just take it.

Maybe I didn't have everything some of the other kids had, but I didn't feel poor. I didn't really think about it. I had a huge front yard and a big pecan tree with a rope swing, and my own wild garden of gorgeous poppies. I knew where the best climbing trees were, and the best roofs too. I knew where the biggest blackberries grew, and a mulberry tree in a vacant lot that nobody else knew about. I could run really fast through the neighborhoods and the park. I wasn't supposed to (because it wasn't ladylike) but I did it anyway. It made me happy, and it didn't cost anything. I went barefoot every day all summer long. I was free to wander anywhere I wanted, and life was full of new adventures and interesting things to discover.

After we moved to East Side, I didn't see Vivian and Dimi as much anymore, they were too far away to walk to. But I'd met a new friend, Patricia, to do things with.

There was an old lady, and Pat and I used to play in her back yard. She seemed nice, and she didn't seem to mind us there. She had a canary in a cage and sometimes we would look in through her back parlor window at it, and listen to it singing. One day we were doing that, and maybe she thought we were snooping or something, anyway this time she came running outside waving a broom and hollering at us and chased us out of the yard. She yelled "Get offa my property! Y'all po' white trash!"

What was she so mad about? We weren't doing anything!

"And don't come around here no more!" She hollered as we took off down the alley. "Or I'm gonna call the Po-lice." She was kind of crazy, so we got out of there as quick as we could.

That surprised me. I'd never thought that I was poor white trash. I'd heard of that, but I didn't know exactly what it was, and it never occurred to me that maybe I was that. I was poor, and I was white. Was I white-trash?

But I didn't believe that, not for one minute, because I secretly believed that I had the blood of aristocracy in my veins, but just nobody knew it. It came down to me from my Kentucky grandmother. And even if it was mostly fantasy, I believed my great-grandparents were *somebody*. And even if that wasn't true, maybe *I could be someday.*

When summer ended and school started again, I got chosen for 6th grade chorus. There were thirty of us, boys and girls. I sang the high harmony part called soprano. Mrs. Campbell the Music teacher taught the chorus after school. She directed us like a symphony conductor, waving her arms in the air as if she was stirring up a cloud of angels, only it was us.

"Lo, how a rose is blooming..." we sang so earnestly, in four-part harmony. *"To show God's love aright... she bore*

to men a savior, when half-spent was ... the... night."

We sang in auditorium programs at school, and even other schools and churches. At Christmas vacation we were asked to sing on the radio! But I got the flu, and I was so sick. I begged Mama, "Please, please, PLEASE let me go! I've GOT to go. We're going to be on the RADIO!"

"I know, honey," she said. She always called me honey when she was going to say No to something. "But you're sick and it's all the way across town on the bus."

"Daddy said he could take me in the car." I pleaded, and even though my head was pounding and spinning in a fog, I said, "I feel much better today," It didn't fool her one bit. "We'll see." she said.

I lay in my bed barely conscious for three more days. I wasn't getting any better. I gazed through the blur of headache and half-sleep at my sparkling white choir robe, all crisply-starched and ironed, hanging on the outside of the closet door to keep it from crushing.

I've got to go. I've just GOT to!

When the day came, I got up and took a shower. I washed my hair and the steam opened up my nose a little. By a miracle, Mama let me go, and stayed and sat with the other parents. I don't remember much about the concert. I was in the back row on the highest riser and I had to concentrate on not falling off. I was dizzy and a little bit nauseous, but once the program started, I forgot about that. I don't think I sang very well, but I was there! I was on the radio! Afterward I actually did feel better.

I loved singing. It was like floating on sheer joy. It was magical. We were just a bunch of kids, but our voices were sincere and clear and true. Mrs. Campbell taught us to sing the word "God" with a round, full, deep "O" instead of "Gahd." She received our sweet Texas-twangy child-voices with love and respect, and shaped them into the sounds of her choir of angels.

Nothing else I had ever done had ever lifted me up like that, from what I thought I was, to where I experienced what I could be. Sixth grade chorus gave me a feeling I didn't get at home. It made me One Of Us, and I mattered. Singing gave me the absolute joy of lifting my voice in a glorious way with all the others, and then we became more than ourselves, we became music.

I was living in a troubled and confused time then, with a brother who hated me and a mother whose life was crumbling into divorce, alcoholism, and loss of faith. There was no closeness in what was left of our family. We were living in poverty which I was secretly ashamed of, and I didn't have much more to hope for. But when I sang, I felt different. I was somebody that had a real worth somehow. Mrs. Campbell smiled at us. We were special. For a little while, the possible-me flowed out and joined the voices of other kids like me, and that changed us.

It was a hot weekend in May when Mama got the letter in the mail. Not much fuss was made over the news. Mama and Daddy were still separated upstairs and downstairs and not talking to each other. In a way, all of us were separated and nobody knew what to do. When she called me in from the yard to tell me, she was very quiet. Her eyes looked red like she'd been crying, but her voice was calm when she told me that my Granny had died. That's all she said.

I took the news in silence too. I didn't know what to say. I didn't know what to feel except kind of sad and empty. It meant Granny wasn't coming back anymore. I stood there for a long awkward time, and finally Mama said, almost in a whisper, "Go back out and play now."

I went outside and sat down in the middle of the yard in the lush green grass. I tried to imagine how to feel about the news that my Granny had died. That *anyone* had died. *What does that mean?* I felt sadness, but it was a floating thing; it didn't have anything to hold on to.

I was twelve and I had not seen Granny since I was nine or ten, when she left to go back to North Carolina and Daddy said she couldn't come back here anymore. I think that tore away a part of me, and now the news, that she had died, fell onto old scars that didn't know how to feel any new pain. I just knew that she was gone, and I hoped she was up there in the sky with God, like she told me. I comforted myself with knowing that now her poor old knees wouldn't hurt her every night anymore. I had no real concept of God or heaven. Most of what I'd heard seemed like a fairy tale. Now all I could feel was a deep sense of loneliness and peacefulness. I didn't know how to feel anything else.

There in the yard, everything looked beautiful. It was almost summer and my poppies were blooming in the wild foundation-garden, scarlet-red petals fluttering and dancing in the hot breeze. The grass was thick and lush and green. Brilliant light was everywhere, hurting my eyes. I sat in the shade of the big pecan tree feeling sober and very silent for a long time, but I didn't know how to feel sorrow. There was an achy little empty place in me, but that was not new. It came the night she left on the train. Sitting there in the middle of all this beauty and glorious sunshine, I wondered, *How should I feel?* The idea of death seemed so far away, I could almost believe it wasn't true.

My mind wandered to thoughts of the brave wonderful thoroughbred horses that soon, this very day, would run the biggest race of the year, in Lexington where Mama was born. The most amazing horse that year was Native Dancer. He was called "The Grey Ghost" and he had won every race he ran. It was the 1953 Kentucky Derby, and he was the "favorite," the sure bet to win.

I climbed through the window into Daddy's apartment and I turned on the TV set just as the race was starting.

A bell clanged and the gates flew open and the whole row of horses sprang forth at once as if they were shot from slingshots. They charged down the track, thundering along with their legs thrashing fiercely like the devil himself was right behind them.

The horses clumped together in a close pack, fighting for positions near the rail. Somehow Native Dancer got cut off, he was bumped and fouled twice by other horses and slammed against the rail on the first turn. He stumbled, almost knocked off his feet. He lost ground and fell behind, but he didn't give up, he just ran harder.

From the rear of the pack he came pounding his way back up toward the front again, around the outside, coming from way, way back, lunging forward with all his heart and fierce determination, gaining and gaining with incredible strength and speed...

In front of the TV set I held my breath. I felt as if my heart would explode. It was pounding so hard I could feel it shaking my body.

The great horse ran as hard as he could, astonishingly gaining, gaining, pulling closer and closer to the front of the pack, and the crowd of thousands were on their feet, screaming...

Native Dancer came thundering across the finish line, an unbelievably close, heroic. heartbreaking second-place. It was the first race he ever lost in his career.

After the race, I went back out to the yard. I sat in the grass again and thought about my Granny. I wondered what it was like to leave the earth forever and go to live with God. I didn't know much about God, but I hoped He would let her travel if she wanted to, and He would fix it so she was young and strong with good legs that didn't hurt.

My mind drifted back to thoughts about the courage and beauty of the great gray horse who ran with all his heart, and still didn't win the race. Both of those things made me sad, but I kew I couldn't change either one. I let my Granny from Kentucky, out there somewhere, slip away and be free. I knew she wanted me to.

After that, things went on the same old way, just quieter. Fall came and I went back to school. Then one morning something happened. I was just beginning to wake up, still drowsy and warm in my bed when I heard a sound, like a big THUMP in the bathroom hallway, then a little moan or something. I leaned out from my bed and looked around.

It was Mama. She was in the hall, so all I could see was just the top of her head and her hands as she struggled and tried to get up from the floor. Then I heard Tommy there too. He must have been trying to help her get up.

"I'm not drunk" she mumbled. "Charlene must have given me some goofballs. I'm not drunk." Charlene was her girlfriend; they both worked the cocktail shift at the Diamond Horseshoe.

"I took some pills." she said. "Charlene gave me some

pills. They must have been goofballs. I'm not drunk."

It was always awful how she got when she drank too much. I never used to see her like that when we lived at Beacon and Columbia, and it scared me. It was like she was not herself, and it gave me a bad feeling in the pit of my stomach.

I turned away. I wasn't sure what was happening, and for a minute I thought maybe I was dreaming. I slid back under the covers. I could hear her talking to Tommy. Her voice was blurry. I listened and tried to figure it out. It was something like "I spent the night at Charlene's to make Daddy jealous..." Then she and Tommy went and sat on the edge of her bed in plain sight, so I knew I must be awake. It was 7:15. I had to get up and go to school.

Tommy had a funny look on his face like he was angry but sad at the same time. Mama kept on saying "I'm not drunk" in that mumbly voice, and the expression on her face was like somebody who got caught doing something they shouldn't. I had a bad feeling, the kind I always got when something was happening and everybody else knew what it was, and I didn't.

I got up and started to get dressed. Mama looked at me for a second and then she turned back to Tommy. He looked like he was going to cry for a minute, but he didn't. I don't think Tommy ever cried in his whole life. He scrunched his eyebrows together in a very serious look, like he was a grown-up, and he said "I believe you Mama."

All of it was a puzzle to me, but Tommy knew a lot of things I didn't know about. He knew dirty words and other grown-up stuff, and I think he knew what Mama meant. Later I asked him what goofballs were.

"They're pills that make you goofy," he said "like

you're drunk. And if you drink beer with them too, you get double-drunk and you can't walk good." So I figured that was why she fell. She broke her wrist in the fall, and then she couldn't work, so she lost her job.

There were so many other things I didn't understand then, but nobody I could ask. Tommy might have known, but he was a teenage punk, he wanted nothing to do with a kid sister, so we were no help to each other. We were farther apart than ever. If he knew anything, he wasn't going to tell me. I think we both felt like the floor was falling out from under us and we didn't know what to do. Whatever was happening between Mama and Daddy, it must have been going on longer than I thought, even before we moved to East Side.

The divorce came, and all of us moved out of the little house. Daddy moved first. I helped him carry things out to the car from his place downstairs. Mama was upstairs and she was upset. When I went back upstairs she told me the divorce was final, and she asked me whether I wanted to go with her or go with Daddy.

"What?" I stood there dumbfounded.

"Daddy and I are not going to be together anymore," she said, "and you and Tommy will have to say if you want to live with me or live with Daddy." But that was unimaginable, to have to choose.

Then she said, "If you went to live with Daddy, he could do more for you than I could. He could buy you nice things." And she said some more stuff I can't remember now, but I got the message that she was hoping I'd go and live with Daddy, like she was sort of trying to talk me into it. I wasn't too surprised, because she had always liked

Tommy the most, so I answered what I thought she wanted me to say.

Quietly and shyly I said, "I think I would like to live with Daddy." The look on her face told me instantly. That was the wrong answer. She was hurt, and I was very confused. And I thought, *Why do grown-ups say things backwards instead of what they really mean? If they would just say the truth, everything would be so much easier! I wouldn't always have to guess what they meant, and get it wrong!*

Really, she made me get it wrong. I said what I thought she wanted. I didn't mean to hurt her, honest I didn't. But the truth was, I really did want to go with Daddy. He was there during the day studying his correspondence course at the kitchen table, and he let me hang around downstairs with him and draw pictures at his desk. He said my horse drawings were really good. And back when we lived at Beacon and Columbia, he used to take all of us for drives out into the country, then we would stop at the Dairy Queen and have ice cream. I loved that. Then after they were "separated" and Daddy lived downstairs, he took me to see Vivian and Dimi, and sometimes other places with his friends Tut and Dottie, like swimming, and the State Fair. I felt closer to Daddy than to Mama because he was around more, and because he liked me. But in the end, it didn't matter anyway. The court awarded custody of my brother and me to Mama, because in Texas, that was what they usually always did.

Chapter 8: Red Brick Apartment Building

Mama never laughed anymore. The heels were worn-down on her waitress shoes, but she painted them with the chalky white stuff in a bottle so they would look neat and clean. Her waitress uniforms went to the Chinese laundry to get washed and starched and ironed, because the laundromat made everything gray.

I knew something was different as soon as Daddy came back from his trip to see his brother in Arizona. He was quieter. He didn't smile much either, and after we all moved away from the house on East Side Avenue I didn't know where he lived, and I could only see him sometimes on the weekends.

Mama found a new apartment in a red brick building. There wasn't any yard, just the street in front and a gravel parking lot in the back. The apartment was just one real room. The couch was right inside the door and then Mama's bed. There was a space toward the back of the apartment, like a hall, but wider, next to the kitchen like maybe it was supposed to be a dinette area. A bare lightbulb dangled from the ceiling by a twisted electric cord. You pulled a little chain to turn it on, and it gave off a gloomy yellow light, just enough to find your way to the bathroom further down at the end of the hall.

Tommy slept on the rollaway bed in that hall space by the kitchen, and Mama and I slept in her bed, until that guy came. Then I slept on the couch and they slept in the bed.

He was good-looking I guess, anyway he sure thought he was. He was mean to Mama, always telling her what to do. He told Tommy and me they were married, but I don't think it was true. Tommy didn't like him and I didn't like him either. He smiled at me a lot but it was a weird smile, it made me feel uncomfortable.

After he came and I had to sleep on the couch, I didn't mind that, except it was near the bed and I was embarrassed to get undressed in front of him. I had just turned thirteen and I was beginning to get very small buds of breasts. He always looked at me when I got ready to go to bed. I slept in my cotton panties and one of Tommy's old T-shirts, and the way he stared at me made me feel funny, like he shouldn't do that. I couldn't exactly say why, but it felt strange when he looked at me and grinned at me in that creepy way. I think Mama noticed it too. About four days later, he was gone. After that, nobody ever said anything more about it. I don't remember his name.

That was about the time I started finding whiskey bottles in odd places around the apartment, those flat ones like the bums on East Side used to carry in their coat pockets. I found one in the freezer of the fridge once, and another time behind the couch, and one in the bathroom linen cabinet underneath the towels.

The red brick apartment building had eight apartments on two floors. The long hallways were dark and spooky even in the daytime. Our place was on the second floor, all the way in the back. I didn't know where Daddy lived then, but he came and got me sometimes on weekends and took me to see Vivian and Dimi while he talked with Pete and Julia, their dad and mom. We would have dinner there and watch TV, then I would spend the night with Vivian and Dimi, and Daddy would come back for me in the morning. Dr. Pete was Daddy's best friend ever since we came to Texas. Vivian and Dimi called my dad Uncle George and we called their dad Uncle Pete. He was a chiropractor now, and while he went to chiropractic school, they had all lived in a trailer in San Antonio. Now they had a really nice house of their own and it was a really happy place to be. Tommy didn't come. He didn't want to see Daddy. I don't know why.

Vivian and Dimi's Mom and Dad both worked hard too, but they were together, and Vivian and her sister Dimi liked each other. Nobody picked on anybody. They always treated me like I was okay too, sort of like a cousin. Pete and Julia had squabbles once in a while, but they loved each other, they loved their girls, and Daddy and Pete loved each other like brothers.

After a while Daddy met Helen, and then he took me to meet her. We all went to a movie. It was "Funny Face" starring Audrey Hepburn. Helen said she looked like me! I was all arms and legs, dark eyes and awkwardness, and skinny as a toothpick, and she said Audrey Hepburn looked like me! I liked Helen right away.

Summer was ending and I was going to start junior high school in the Fall. I had no idea how to act in that new world. I was thin and gangly and I didn't have any good clothes. Helen took me shopping and bought me some new skirts and blouses, I was amazed. She did it for no reason, just to be nice.

By now Tommy was fifteen. He was running around with a bunch of boys that smoked cigarettes and talked dirty trying to BE somebody. They were not a real gang. They broke into warehouses and people's garages at night and stole things. They taught Tommy how to hot-wire ignitions to start cars without the key. He really bragged about that. Sometimes they would steal a car and drive around until it ran out of gas, then they just left it there.

My brother was smart, but he didn't like school. So sometimes he left school at lunch period and didn't come back, looking for something more interesting to do.

When we lived at the red brick apartment he was gone more, so he didn't hurt me as much, but the silent threat was always there. I didn't hate my brother, but I feared and dreaded him. I didn't even try to tell Mama anymore. I made my pledge to myself every single day, that I would always be as different from him as possible.

That meant I couldn't get mad, and I could never try to defend myself, because that would bring more punishment. I couldn't lie, especially that– because Tommy was such a liar and I didn't want to be like him. He was really a genius liar. He was so clever and charming that people believed him just because they wanted to. No matter how obvious the lie was, he almost always got away with it. The ones I heard the most were: "She's crazy! I never even touched her." or if he got caught, he'd say "It was an accident. I didn't mean to."

The injuries were mostly not too bad, but they made me have to be afraid of him all the time. He taught me that this was my share in life, to be treated like a punching bag for his entertainment, and our family rules said it was okay because he was a boy. But there was one time– just once, that my brother broke his own rules. I never expected that.

I was waiting for Patricia to come out to play, sitting by myself in a little rope swing we had made in the car-port behind the apartment building. It was a stupid swing, made out of some scraggly old jute rope we'd found. It wasn't strong at all. I was sitting in it, swaying a little, not even swinging, when all of a sudden the rope broke. It just snapped – and I hit the ground really hard.

The next thing I knew I was on my back on the gravel in horrible pain and I couldn't breathe. My chest felt like a car ran over it and squashed all the air out. When I tried to suck air in, I couldn't. I struggled desperately to draw a breath, but no matter how hard I tried, no air came in! Instead it was making a strange ugly honking sound. *Honk... honk...*

I couldn't breathe, I couldn't scream, I was terrified, and I was lying there, honking, crazy-wild with panic. Then up the driveway, of all the people in the world, came Tommy.

The first thing he did was kick me in the shoulder with the toe of his sneaker. Not very hard, more like you would nudge a dead squirrel on the pavement to see if it's really dead. All I could do was lie there with a frantic look on my face, desperately trying to breathe. *Honk... honk... honk...*

He said, "Stop that! What's the matter with you?"

I looked up at him with terror in my eyes. *Honk... honk...* I couldn't speak, I could only make the honking noises. *Honk...* I tried so hard to get air, even the littlest bit, into my lungs, *honk...* but I couldn't. He kicked me again.

"What are you doing?" he said. "Stop that! Get up!"

It took several horribly long minutes *honk... honk...* before the honking subsided enough and there was a tiny bit of air in me so that I was able to squeak out the words,

"I can't." *Honk... honk...*

The jarring fall had knocked all the wind out of my lungs and it had done something bad to my back. All I remember was being terrified and desperate to breathe. The kicks didn't matter. I didn't expect him to help me; he was simply irrelevant and it didn't even matter *honk... honk...* that he was standing there, looking down at me, watching me die.

He must have finally realized that I wasn't fooling, and something was really wrong. Then, incredibly, he picked me up and lugged me back to the house, and somehow he got me up the stairs.

I had injured my spine. For days, the agony in my back continued at full fury without any relief. I lay in the bed, whimpering in pain all day and all night for four days, and finally Mama told Daddy and he took me to see Dr. Pete at his chiropractor office.

Dr. Pete put me on the hard black table and with his strong hands, he did a sort of hip-twist movement of me that played my whole spine like a xylophone. Wth a series of musical pops and clicks, my bones obeyed, and the pain stopped.

Later I would always wonder, *Did Tommy really do that to help me?* I always thought so. There must have been a little bit of compassion in him. Not love maybe, but something. He could have just laughed and walked away as usual, but that time he didn't. He didn't walk away.

Daddy had met Helen at the Greater Dallas Club where he worked. She worked part-time on the switchboard two weekends a month, the times when her ex-husband took her little girls to visit his parents in Conroe Texas. She was divorced too, so I think it was like how Daddy took me on the weekend sometimes, Sam took Mary and Martha. Helen worked full time at State Farm Insurance Company and extra part time at the Country Club to support herself and her girls. By then, Daddy had worked his way up to Maître d' at the club.

My Daddy was very handsome. He had thick black hair and dark brown eyes, Greek eyes, where his soul showed through. He knew how to be dignified. He didn't own the tuxedo he wore at work, but he looked very elegant in it. He looked like Gregory Peck in the movies.

Helen liked him, and he liked her too. She had sparkling blue eyes, as bright as his were dark, and I think she was enchanted by his polite refined manner. Enchanted was my favorite new word. It means you think somebody is really wonderful. I didn't know it then, and maybe they didn't know it either, but I think they were falling in love.

Daddy started bringing me to Helen's house for the weekends. She taught me to make baking-powder biscuits from scratch. I got dusty clouds of flour all over her kitchen floor, but she didn't mind, and the biscuits were fabulous. Her girls were eight and ten and I was thirteen, just about right for playmates.

It was one of those Sunday nights when I came back from a weekend visit with Daddy. I had stayed at Helen's house, and her girls and I played together like sisters all day long till dinnertime. Then Daddy came and we all had dinner together, and that was the best part. It was a perfect day.

I was feeling tired and happy when Daddy dropped me off in front of the red brick apartment building at ten o'clock and watched until I was safely inside before he drove away.

In the first-floor hallway I flipped the light-switch on, the kind that only stays on for a quick minute and then goes out all by itself, and you have to walk the rest of the way in the dark. It went out. In pitch black I climbed the stairs to the second floor to our apartment. I fished in my pocket for my key and I noticed the door was not quite closed. I pushed it open and went in.

Tommy was standing just inside the door. He must have got home a minute before me. When I stepped through the door he grabbed me by the shoulders and spun me around toward the window.

"Don't look!" he said.

The window blinds were closed; there was nothing to look at. I wondered, *What in the world is he doing?*

"Don't look at what?" and I turned to look over my shoulder, and then I saw it.

A strange ugly man, an old guy, is coming out of our bathroom at the other end of the apartment, walking toward us. The hall-space behind him is flooded with the dim yellow light from the bare bulb hanging from the ceiling. Even in the shadows I can see that he is naked, and I can see his thing.

Behind him, just a second later, Mama came out of the bathroom and she was naked too. When she saw Tommy and me standing there, she stopped suddenly and dashed back into the bathroom.

When the man saw us, he muttered some cuss-words. He grabbed his clothes off the bed and hurried to put them on. Then with his shoes in his hand and still cursing at us, he shoved me and Tommy out of his way and went out the door.

We both stood there frozen to the spot. Mama came back out, wearing her bathrobe. The apartment was dark except for the dull yellow light from the hall-space light bulb. I had walked into something I couldn't understand.

"Who was that man? What was he doing here?"
Mama dropped herself into the chair and started to cry.

"Please forgive me!" she said. "I didn't do anything.

Please forgive me!" My mind reeled. *What is happening?*

It was like one of those nightmares where strange things that can't really happen are happening. *Like you're falling off a cliff into the ocean, and you know it's a dream but you can't wake up, so you can't stop yourself from falling.*

She had been drinking. She looked awful. I'd seen her like that before, but it was worse this time. She was somebody I didn't even know.

Like when you see a car crash on the highway and you stare at it. You don't want to see it, but you can't make yourself look away.

Mama kept saying the same thing, "Please forgive me... I didn't do anything. Please forgive me." But that didn't make any sense. I tried to figure it out, but I couldn't.

If she didn't do anything, why is she saying please forgive me? What is it that she didn't do? And what was that awful man doing here? Why were they walking around in the dark, naked?

I was shocked and confused. I was mad at her for being drunk, and yet I was sad for her too. Sad that she was like this, and I knew she couldn't help it, and I couldn't help her either. She was helpless and I was helpless and Tommy was helpless and there we all were, and she just kept on saying it, "Please forgive me. I didn't do anything. Please forgive me."

There was a sort of ringing in my ears, and then, all of a sudden, everything went still. Like the film broke and the movie stopped. I felt completely calm.

This is not really real...

All of a sudden it was like nothing mattered anymore.

In the hall-space, the lightbulb was swinging gently on its cord, making the shadows on the walls sway slowly back and forth. Then everything started to fade away, like it was all dissolving into the dirty yellow light.

I sat down in the living room on a dinette chair. Tommy was sitting on the couch in the dark at the edge of the dim light from the hall. I couldn't see his face. The long shadows flowed across the floor like muddy water.

I was looking at the floor under the chair where Mama sat leaning toward us, half in shadow, half in light. She was saying something to us, trying to explain, but now her voice seemed very far away.

I'm dreaming this. I will wake up, and this will go away.

I felt my mind and my body come apart, and then they were sanding there, side by side, two different things, silently watching us, watching everything. They were both me, but not me.

I am not here, and this is not my life.

The apartment door was still open and a cold draft from the hallway seeped in. Mama pulled her bathrobe tighter around her. She was still saying it.

"Please forgive me... I didn't do anything... Please forgive me." Her eyes were puffy and her hair was all frowsy. She didn't look pretty. I hated to see her like that. She was different when she drank. She changed, and it scared me.

Beneath Mama's chair there was a trail of ants, winding silently across the floor. I sat perfectly still, staring at them. They were crossing over stripes of shadows on the floor, yellow and black, yellow and black.

The long column of ants was moving steadily from the kitchen behind the refrigerator, then under Mama's chair where the dirty yellow light slanted across the floorboards, and then into the darkness of the front room. I watched them marching all in a line like a tiny army.

I didn't say anything. I don't think Tommy said anything either. If he did, I didn't hear. I sat absolutely still, absolutely quiet. Mama was still saying it, "Please forgive me," but it didn't matter anymore, and everywhere beyond the circle of sickly yellow light, there was darkness.

I'm not really here, I am far away.

I gazed at the little dotted-line of ants under Mama's chair. The shadows from the yellow light made the cracks between the floor-boards look like rows of ink lines from a pen. Everything else went away. I heard her voice, but she was somewhere off in the distance. It was late. I was so tired. I just wanted to sleep, to go away, and forget.

I'm not here. My body is here, but I'm not. If I wanted to, I could fly away and never come back.

The caravan of ants were hurrying in both directions, passing each other all along a crawling crooked black line in their own tiny world, unaware of us. Mama was still saying it. Nothing made any sense. I couldn't understand. I wondered if Tommy did. He was sitting there in the shadows, looking down at the floor too.

Soon after that night, we had to move again. This time it was to a falling-down old place I called the haunted house. There wasn't much to move this time. Mama had sold the cedar chest and the twin beds, back when we left East Side Avenue. I don't remember moving day. That year there were gaps of time that I can't remember at all.

She was still a young woman, broke and lonely. She was drowning. I knew it, but I had no way to comprehend it. Her life was pulling her down but I didn't know what to do. I thought it must be my fault. I wanted to help her but I couldn't.

Memory has its own rules. Time expands or contracts illogically. We selectively forget, or maybe some protective function in us forgets. It files some things away in a dusty steel file-drawer locked with a key, and then hides the key.

Of the worst times we remember only the chalk outlines, the fact that they happened. If there is something too painful, the mind walls-off that part. The most damaging events, especially in childhood, may be mercifully hidden for decades, or forever.

There are some spaces in my remembering where the chronology is broken with a dotted line. The haunted house was one of those. I have very little memory of it. I only know that it was the darkest, loneliest time for all of us. This is what I remember:

It was a boarded-up abandoned house. It might have been condemned. I called it the haunted house because it was so desolate and forlorn, and it looked like it had been empty for a long time. Part of it was overgrown with weeds and vines that were slowly dragging it down. The front door and windows were boarded up with plywood, but we could get in through the back door where weeds and brambles over the porch kept it hidden from the street. The house was set back from a windblown vacant lot. The grass was grey and the house was grey, so if you didn't know it was there, you would never notice it from the street.

The back door was the only opening. We sneaked in and

out. You had to slip through a gap in the dense mat of creeper grass and dead morning-glory vines that covered the falling-down wooden back porch, then past a crooked screen-door stuck halfway open so it couldn't either open or close. Then a deadbolt door into the kitchen.

An elderly woman friend of Mama's was letting us stay there because we had no place to live and it was winter. Somehow she got the water, gas, and electricity turned on, but it was still cold. Some of the windows were broken and there were holes in the roof that dripped rain. There was a little gas heater in one room, so I stayed right next to it as much as possible. That was where I slept, on the squeaky old rusty roll-away bed. Then there was Mama's room. It had a closet. All of our clothes were there. They didn't take up much room. I can't remember where Tommy slept. I don't remember seeing him or Mama during that time, though they lived there too.

Inside the house it was always dark, but a little bit of pale sunlight filtered through at the upper part of the dust-caked windowpanes where the boards didn't reach.

At night the wind moaned through the broken glass and the cold seeped and bled through the walls and window casings, even with the plywood over them. My bed was a few feet from the little gas stove, but still the mattress was like a slab of ice every night. I plugged in the iron and ran it back and forth over the sheet. The heat didn't last, but it helped with the first icy plunge under the covers.

We must not have been there very long, a few weeks, or a few months. I can't remember. When I try to go back, there are only blank spaces. I didn't know where Tommy was, or Mama either. When she broke her wrist before we left East Side Avenue, she had lost her waitress job at the bar, so she was probably out looking for another job. Those were desolate times for all of us, They must have been terrible times for Mama.

I had just started junior high school that Fall, timid and mostly bewildered. I didn't know what to do or how to be. It was a big step of growing up, and I knew I was not ready for it. I needed a mother and a full-time father, but I didn't have that, and I didn't know why. That was just the way it was. It might have helped to have a brother I could talk to, at least we would have been in it together, but I didn't have that either. For Mama, I guess the drinking helped her to keep going, but really it was making everything worse. She was sinking deeper and deeper.

Daddy had never much cared to drink, except egg-nog at Christmas, though he knew all kinds of fancy drinks from being a bartender. That was how he got that good waiter-job at the country club. There was a want-ad for a part-time bartender, so he got a library book and taught himself how to mix fancy drinks. It wasn't what he wanted, but it was better than what he'd had. Daddy was looking for a new start. Over the last few years he had studied and earned a GED high school equivalency diploma and then he finished the electronics repair correspondence course. He wanted a new kind of job and a different kind of life.

Mama was still trying to hang on to the life that was gone. The alcohol was dragging her down, and there was nothing any of us could do about it. Tommy was roaming around at night with his gang of boys getting in trouble with the law. I never saw them though, he never brought any friend home to anyplace we lived. The haunted house was lonely for me, but it probably was easier for me than Mama and Tommy. Of the three of us, I was the least lost. I was used to being alone, so I knew how.

One morning in the middle of October I left the house to go to school. A freezing rain had fallen and there was frost and ice on the ground. My shoes crunched across the frozen grass of the vacant lot and when I reached the sidewalk it was a sheet of ice. I skittered carefully down the walk toward the street, and then I saw Daddy's car parked there. He and Helen were in it. Daddy had never come there before, I hadn't seen him ever since we moved from the red brick apartment. He called to me so I walked over.

Daddy said "Get in the car, Vickie." So I did. It was nice and warm in there. Helen smiled kindly, though she looked worried. She was looking at the boarded-up house. Daddy asked me if Tommy had left for school yet, and if Ann, Mama, was inside the house. I told him no, she wasn't, and Tommy wasn't either.

"Would it be all right if we came in the house?" Helen asked me hesitantly and very politely.

I said "I guess so." I had no idea what was happening, but something was. Both of them looked kind of serious.

I led them back to the house and the three of us went crunching through the frozen grass again to the back porch and the hidden kitchen door. Nobody said anything.

We went inside. Helen and Daddy walked through the rooms, Helen first. Daddy seemed nervous, but Helen was not afraid. In the kitchen she opened the fridge. The rusty racks were empty except for the ketchup, one beer, and half a case of stolen Cola from Tommy's last warehouse raid. She stood there a minute. A small sound escaped her. Was it a sigh? Or a word? I couldn't tell.

In the room where I slept it was dark. The flames in the little gas heater sputtered and murmured but the room was still cold. We could see our breath. My bed was there next to the heater, rumpled and unmade. I was embarrassed. I had never thought anyone would see it.

We went into Mama's room. Neatly hung in the closet were the things Helen had bought for me, Ann's waitress uniforms, and a few other things I can't remember.

"Oh, George," she said softly. He touched her arm gently. She pulled a little handkerchief out of her coat-pocket and dabbed her eyes. They looked at each other in silence for a moment, a long moment.

They sent me out to the car so they could talk. When they came back out, the decision must have been made in those few minutes. I think when Helen saw the way we lived, she couldn't leave me there. Not another day, not another minute. Her mind was made up, and as I would soon come to know, once her mind was made up, God was at her elbow, and her cause could not be defeated by anything on earth.

Back outside in the car we sat together. They asked me, "Where is your brother?"

"I don't know. I haven't seen him for a while."

"Do you know where he might be?"

"No."

With that, Daddy and Helen looked at each other again. There was something happening, a communication between them that wasn't in words. Helen had tears in her eyes, but she was strong; she held them there. I felt very awkward.

"I'm going to miss the bus. "I'll be late for school."

"Don't worry," Helen said. "We'll take you to school."

We went back into the house and gathered my things and came back out carrying my clothes and belongings in two paper grocery bags, and then we drove to the junior high school.

I sat on a hard straight-back wooden chair outside the principal's office waiting, wondering if I was in trouble, while they talked to the principal and filled out paperwork. In less than an hour they had signed me out of school, and then we went to Helen's house and they made arrangements to enroll me in a new school, T.J. Rusk Junior High.

Technically, they had kidnapped me. They took me from there with not much more than the clothes on my back. I would never see that place again. In the space of one day, my old life was over forever, and my new life began.

At Helen's house the rest of the day, the hours flew by with a whirlwind of wonders. When Helen said I was going to stay there, I went dizzy with amazement. Evening came, and dinner. So much food! Hot and steamy, and so good! Meatloaf and lima beans and mashed potatoes and gravy. I ate a whole plate full and even had seconds.

That night I lay blissfully warm under clean sheets and soft blankets on Helen's couch, so wonderfully cozy next to the big heater in the living room. I loved the warm, I soaked it up, all the way to my bones. I was tired but excited too, and still completely astonished. I gazed at the lovely red glow of the stove and drifted into sleep, feeling so safe, and happier than I had ever been in my life.

Chapter 9: Stigall Street

In the morning when my eyes opened, a pale early light was pouring through a window with flowered drapes. I gazed around the room. There was the big old console Motorola TV with a crocheted doily on top of it, and the comfy old brown chair next to the heater. *I am in Helen's house.*

I closed my eyes, squeezed them shut tight, and then opened them again to see if all of it would still be there. It was. *It's not a dream. I'm really here.*

From the kitchen came small sounds of clinking and clatter and the smell of biscuits baking. Helen's cheerful voice chirped from the hallway, "Wake up girls, breakfast in five minutes!" And then I heard the chattering voices of my new sisters Mary Beth and Martha from their room just a few steps away, the room that would soon be mine too, after the addition of another bunk-bed.

It would be a few days before they found my brother, and then another three weeks to get him released from Juvenile Hall, the County lockup for adolescent offenders. He'd been caught with a stolen car and arrested again.

I didn't know it then, but Tommy and I were a big part of the reason why Daddy and Helen decided to get married, when they had known each other for less than a year. She never told me until long after I was grown how scared she was when they made the decision. I'm sure Daddy was too. But she couldn't leave me and Tommy like that, in that boarded-up house, and she did love my handsome quiet Dad very much. They took a chance and started a new life together. It was a heroic act for them both.

After the divorce, all of us had left the house on East

Side Avenue. Daddy moved someplace else and I didn't know where. Mama and Tommy and I had moved to the red brick apartment building and then after a few months we had to move again, this time to the haunted house. I hardly ever saw either Mama or Tommy after that. All three of us were pretty much alone and lost.

Only Daddy had been still hopeful, still seeking a better life. When he found it, the woman he loved brought me and my brother into that new life too, because she loved my father that much, and because she was an extraordinary woman. She brought two teenagers into her home and into her life, one she'd never met, and both, she knew, were emotionally scarred. She took the risk that there could be enough love for this courageous venture to work.

At three months short of fourteen, I was not fully aware of what a momentous thing this was. I just did what I was told, blissfully happy to do it. If I'd had all the wishes of Aladdin, I couldn't have chosen a more wonderful thing. The loneliness was over, God's grace like a thunderbolt had given me a home and a full-time mother and father and two new sisters in the bargain! There would be adjustments to make for all of us the next few years, but for the first time in a very long time, I was wanted. I was in a place that was my place to be, and I had been given the right to be there.

And there was more good news. The bullying and intimidation from my brother would now come to an abrupt halt. Helen did not allow any of that in her house. Suddenly I was safe. I didn't have to be afraid anymore.

Helen must have had a thousand things to do before the wedding, working full-time on the switchboard at State Farm Insurance and raising her two daughters. Now she had three, and a son too. Still she managed to squeeze in enough time for me. I didn't have anything nice to wear to the wedding, so she took me on a shopping trip. One of her many practical talents was finding bargains, a sport of skill and ingenuity, and Helen was a world-class pro.

She had me trying on dresses at J.C. Penney's. I put on one pretty dress after another in the tiny dressing room and then came out to show her. I felt like a fashion model.

"Turn around" she said, "let me see how you look." I whirled, she adjusted sleeves and shoulder seams. Most things that were small enough for me, the sleeves were too short and my awkward wrists dangled out. But finally the perfect dress was found. Dusty pink, princess waistline, a simple scoop neckline and cap sleeves. I was flushed with happiness. All of this was so new and unbelievable, it made my head spin.

Next came the shoe department. She picked some styles for me to try on, and finally chose simple pumps with tiny high heels like Audrey Hepburn wore in Funny Face. I'd never felt so elegant in my whole life.

I didn't have a coat, just a corduroy jacket, and it was a boy's jacket. Helen's close friend Hazel gave her a soft three-quarter length cream-colored wool coat for me, handed down from her daughter Jenny, and it fit me perfectly.

Things fell into place, and when the wedding day came, all of Daddy's women looked lovely. Mary Beth, Martha, me, and Helen his radiantly beautiful bride. Truly there was a light shining around her. She wore a simple full-skirted day-length dress that flowed gracefully over her full hips and gently hugged her small waist. It was periwinkle blue, the color of her eyes. Daddy wore his best suit, and all of us trooped off to University Park Methodist Church where on Saturday, November 13, we became a family for life.

It was a very small wedding, just Helen's closest friends Hazel and Charles Moore, who stood up with them as Best Man and Matron of Honor. Reverend Alsie H. Carleton was the minister. Only Tommy was missing, but he would be out of jail by Thanksgiving and then he too would be brought home.

In the first picture Helen ever took of us, Tommy and I are standing where she has posed us near the rosebushes in the yard of the house on Stigall Street. It's a bright Sunday morning in winter and we are dressed up to go to church. I remember her saying to Tommy encouragingly in her sweet cheerful voice,

"Tom, put your arm around your sister – show her you love her." She called him Tom, not Tommy. He was nearly sixteen, and this was an expression of respect for him as a young man. In the snapshot I look relaxed and happy, smiling shyly but beamingly. Tommy's hand on my shoulder is as stiff as a lobster claw. He is not looking at either Helen or me. He is looking away with a frowning face that is neither a boy's nor a man's, but something uncomfortably in-between. The sleeves of his jacket are a little too short. It was borrowed. He stands tense, rigid, and ramrod straight. He is tall, and already handsome.

We both stood at the threshold of our new life, and I was happy as a lark. Tommy was not. He had lost a lot – his gang, his unrestricted freedom, and his "personal punching bag." My brother's former position of superiority and power had vanished, and to make matters worse, he was now outnumbered by females. His glory days had ended and there was not much he could do about it.

In the first few years of our new life there would be some turbulent moments adjusting to the new experiences, but we survived them and we became a solid family. Helen was a strong and dedicated woman, and that was what Daddy needed. That was what we all needed. I can't recall exactly when I first began to call her Mother instead of Helen, but it came soon, and lasted forever.

On Stigall Street the days were full and busy and happy. Mother was teaching me so many new things. She was a brilliant organizer, planning, coaxing, and reminding. She made sure all our homework was done, baths were taken, and school clothes were laid out for the next day each evening before we went to bed. After school my sisters and I rushed home to watch Mickey Mouse Club and American Bandstand before we started our part of preparing dinner. Every Sunday morning Mother got all of us up, fed, washed and dressed, and off to Church together.

Mother and Daddy loved and cherished each other. They were working-partners who believed that anything was possible with hard work and a lot of faith, and I came to believe it too. Like most American families in the 1950's, we were cheerfully and persistently optimistic. We took a positive outlook, hopeful that the future would only get better. That winter I would turn fourteen.

When I started in the new school, Mary Frances Butler was my first new friend. We took Home Ec sewing classes together, studied together, went to the library and puzzled over the Dewey Decimal System together. After school and weekends we would lie on our bellies across her bedspread looking at "Seventeen" magazine, turning the pages slowly and searching every inch of every page for clues, Social Do's and Don'ts, how to dress, and of course, how to be popular and pretty. We were neither, but we were not the least bit worried about it yet. Her mom made the very best roast beef sandwiches on earth. Almost nothing in their house came out of a box or a can or plastic wrap. I hung out at her house a lot, or she hung out at mine. Summers we made hand-churned fresh peach ice cream. Her mom would set it up, mix the cream and sugar and chunks of fresh peaches and put it into the churn with ice and rock-salt on top. We did the rest. We took turns cranking the churn on the back porch while her older brother and his friend Art tinkered with mysterious car engine things in the garage.

In a snapshot Mary Frances and I we are standing in front of her house, dressed in Capri pants and matching plaid shirts we had sewed ourselves. Both of us are tall and skinny, our gangly wrists hang awkwardly from the sleeves. We are going to the movies, or the State Fair, or shopping at Inwood Shopping Center. We are holding hands. We are not gay, we don't even know what that is. We are simply thirteen, that brief time in life when sister-love is strong and loyal and unquestionably normal.

Weekdays my Mary Beth and I always started dinner with help by phone from Mother at the switchboard, her job at State Farm Insurance. By the time she and Daddy got home, dinner was underway and the table was set.

The dining room was small. When all six of us sat down at the table with both the drop-leaf sections opened up, we filled the room to the walls and the sideboard where Mother kept her treasured few pieces of her grandmother's genuine Havilland china, which would be used only at holidays like Christmas and Thanksgiving. The rest of the year we used indestructible plastic Melamine-ware.

After dinner Mary Beth and I washed the dishes, taking turns at washing or drying. Martha helped clear the table and swept the kitchen floor. With lots of laughing and messing around, we eventually got everything clean and put away. Then we could go into the living room and watch Ed Sullivan and I Love Lucy with Mother and Daddy.

Sundays Daddy always cooked. In the summer it was barbecue chicken roasted on a spit he built, or maybe his special burgers. We ate at the picnic table in the back yard next to the pretty grapevine on the fence. At he peak of summer, Daddy used the tender leaves to wrap dolmathes, and Mother made green grape jelly that lasted through the fall. In winter Daddy made Greek family recipes he learned from his parents in their little restaurant in New Jersey when he was a child. My father was a fantastic cook. That might have bothered some wives, but not Mother. She took pride in her man's talent, and bragged about it.

Mother was always a lady, but she was as strong as she was graceful. If there was anything on earth she feared, it didn't show. Once she set her mind on something, she never let anything stop her, no matter how impossible it seemed at first. She had the courage of her convictions, and was never afraid to face a challenge. From her I learned a quiet, rock-solid faith, not from any one lesson, but by seeing her life and her character every day. She walked the walk.

If she had any flaw at all, maybe it was that she cared about appearances, style and tradition. "But don't just look good," she said, "Be good. When you do anything, do your best." That meant integrity and honesty in thought and deed. "But it doesn't hurt to look nice while you're doing it," she said.

My brother had never liked me, and nothing was going to change that. He had never had any interest in me except for somebody to hold captive with constant fear and dread. When Helen disallowed all of that, I was delighted, I was a soul set free! I didn't even notice my brother's sullen silence. I was totally happy to have a family, wonderful food, and a safe warm place to sleep.

In the old life, he had been a tough guy, a rebel, a high and mighty somebody. Now he'd lost all that, lost his source of pride and power, and worst of all, he'd lost what was left of Mama. She had loved him more than anything, and believed in him no matter what. Decades later in a letter to me, she spoke touchingly about the last time she saw him, when she and Daddy both had to appear to sign him out of jail.

"He wanted to quit school and stay with me and get a job" she wrote. "I was so proud of him for that, but I couldn't let him make that sacrifice for me."

The truth was that he had been expelled from school repeatedly, and when the law caught up with him and his buddies stealing cars, he landed in juvenile jail a few times. For him, leaving school probably looked like the best way out of a bad situation. He was nearly sixteen, able-bodied and strong; maybe he could have gotten some kind of a job. Keeping it though, would have been in some doubt. But there was no doubt about one thing: Helen had saved his life just as surely as she had saved mine.

Chapter 10: In My Mother's House

In Mother's house, Tom's acting-out had to go, but it didn't go willingly. A troubled teenager on the edge of manhood, he was carrying a load of unspoken unresolved resentment and rage against any form of authority.

My brother and I were less than a year apart in school because he had failed too many classes and had too many absences, His first year in the new high school, he still cut classes and played pranks. He loved to show off and get attention.

At lunch period when most of the kids were outside on the school grounds, he had a spectacular trick. He was a fire-eater. He filled his mouth with lighter fluid, lit a match, then he spewed out the fuel in a fine misting spray. The instant the fuel met the match flame, it burst into a big cloud of fire. It was very impressive, always drew a crowd, and everybody applauded. Then one day somebody made him laugh at just the wrong moment and the lighter fluid dribbled down his chin and onto his shirt. When the flame-cloud exploded, his shirt caught fire and his face was burned. When the principal found out about the trick, he got expelled and suspended.

This was not the first time Mother had come to his defense at the Principal's office, and it would not be the last, but she believed he deserved another chance. Mother always stood up for all of us. All of us were her own, there were no "step" children in my mother's house.

Mother bailed him out. She didn't condone his behavior, but she stood by him and directly to the principal, who turned out to be an unusual man. She argued that her son had a troubled past, and convinced him not only to reprieve Tom for his violations, but also to help and mentor him.

Principal Stroud sponsored Tom to get into the Civil Air Patrol, an organization for teens and young adults. It was a civilian volunteer auxiliary of the US Air Force where they learned about airplanes and military careers. It was called the C.A.P. and the teens were called cadets. Tom had loved airplanes ever since he was eleven when he built models of fighter planes. He knew the names and could recognize the profiles of every German, British, and American fighter plane in world war II.

The C.A.P. had training meetings one night a week and field trips one Saturday a month. Mr. Stroud thought this group might help Tom develop pride and self-discipline, so Mother somehow found the money for his uniform.

The first field trip was to search for a man who had jumped out of an airplane and his parachute didn't open. Tom said "We found him lying face down. He was kind of flat, and imbedded about six inches into the ground." I didn't know if he was telling the truth, but it made the C.A.P. sound like a very interesting thing.

Not interesting enough for him though, because after a few months, he and another cadet stole a small plane from there and flew it around Grapevine and Carrollton and some other small towns and then landed it in a mowed field. The sheriff's deputies were waiting for them when they came down. Both of them got kicked out, and that was the end of Tom's Civil Air Patrol career.

He knew he would get caught of course. He was never really afraid of that, it was almost like he wanted to. It got him attention from adults and admiration from other boys. Mother and Daddy were able to keep him out of jail that time, but he was in the doghouse with Mother. She really laid down the law that these foolish pranks were over. He cleaned up his act after that, and didn't get into any more trouble at school. He still skipped class occasionally or failed a test, but mostly he applied himself to the new role of not-a-rebel. He was put back again for missed classes and failed tests, but his grades came up and he got more popular too. Eventually we both graduated, the same year. Nobody in the senior class knew he was two years older, they just thought we were twins.

Girls growing up in Texas had to be pretty, a certain kind of pretty: blue eyes, curly blonde or light-brown hair, full pouty lips, and a cute small turned-up nose. By then my hair was chocolate brown, which was only okay if the rest of you was perfect. I wasn't. My eyes were dark brown like Daddy's and people said I was "attractive," and I hated that. It was a nice way to say not-hopeless but also not-pretty. And even though Audrey Hepburn had made my thin body acceptable and my hair okay, my "Greek" nose, which Mother said was elegant, would not be in style until many years later when Cher came along.

If you didn't match the standard, you had less chances of success in life. I envied my friend Vivian, she was pretty. I wasn't entirely hopeless, but I had Daddy's thin lips and my nose was definitely wrong. In a Texas high school, if you were not a beauty, your options were limited. You either had to accept a lower rank in life, or else you had to have something extra to compensate for your lack.

Except for cheerleader and high-kick drill team, sports for girls were disparaged as (whispered) queer. Running was not a sport for girls at all. The only choices left for girls like me were either to become a "brain," or else have a talent. That was how I became The Artist of my school.

My junior year I was the set-designer for the senior play "Carousel," in charge of a crew of students to build and paint the stage sets. The sponsor was our art teacher Marion Cole. I doubt that I was any better at this than anybody else, but I was the one that had the moxie to volunteer. Miss Cole was a wonderful mentor, and mostly because of her, I got through it all, looking like a winner. The opportunity gave me what every high school kid needs most: an identity. I was president of the Art Service Club, staff artist on the yearbook, and incredibly, in my senior year I was voted "Most Creative" by the student body.

In Helen's care we all grew, but Daddy grew the most. Although he had quit school to join the Navy at seventeen, he had always believed in education. The time he had invested in getting a GED and all those afternoons studying the electronics correspondence course at the kitchen table on East Side Avenue now served him well. He got a job in electronics repair and he left bartender and waiter jobs behind him for good.

Money was always tight, but Mother knew how to stretch a dollar till it cried for mercy. Daddy had never made much money but he was always conscientious with what he had, and maintained a perfect credit record. They both worked hard, and we kids helped at home. Together we all managed to survive and even thrive.

For the senior prom I designed my own dress, inspired by the artist Toulouse-Lautrec's paintings and posters of the Moulin Rouge. It was floor-length white satin, with a short black lace jacket that had a scalloped-edged neckline in front and dipped very low in back. Mother and Vivian's mother Julia constructed it for me. Julia was a master seamstress who had worked on everything from women's business suits to ball gowns and wedding dresses in the alterations department of Neiman-Marcus, the very pricey department store, and she was brilliant at her craft.

The other girls wore fairy-dresses of fluffy nylon net in pastel colors with long white gloves. For my Montmartre look, I wore white satin and black lace, with long black gloves, with my dark hair upswept into a stunning formal coiffure created by Mother. I looked as if I had just stepped out of the pages of Paris Vogue magazine.

At the prom my date, a blind date set up by my brother, was a terrible dancer. He even stepped on the hem of my dress in the Grand March. It was ballroom dancing, and he had absolutely no idea what to do. He'd been drinking, and the night seemed dismally doomed.

But then... I danced one dance with Roland. He was the son of Mother's best friend who lived at the other end of the block on Stigall Street. Roland was older than me, good-looking and way out of my league. My best friend Mary Frances didn't have a date for the prom, so Mother suggested that I should ask Roland to take her. It felt very awkward and I was embarrassed, but I did it. He was a really sweet guy, and he most kindly did take her to the prom.

As I sat at a table looking glum, Roland, gentleman that he was, must have felt sorry for me and he asked me very politely, to dance.

We flowed across the floor as gracefully as Fred Astaire and Ginger Rogers. Even though ballroom dancing was an old-fashioned thing that not many young men knew how to do, he was really good at it. He was tall and handsome too, and I was wishing I could have asked him to the prom for myself, but of course, that would have been unthinkable.

In the end my good deed was rewarded. A few days later, Roland asked me out and took me to the rest of the senior graduation parties and events.

We danced all summer long and everybody thought we would get married, it was just a matter of time. But then he got drafted and had to go to Vietnam, and I went off to college to study art, and everything changed.

My mother's house was no mansion. It was a tiny wood-frame house in a middle-class neighborhood, with rambling roses climbing the porch and a mimosa tree in the front yard. She kept it immaculately neat and clean, and she made room there for all of us.

When Yaiya came to visit there were seven of us to cook for and find beds for, and we all shared one little Frigidaire and a closet-sized bathroom– the busiest place in the house. Somehow she made it all work, with humor and cheerfulness and grace. There was enough, and there was love. As I found myself included in that love, immersed in it, all the starving parts of me began to bloom like a field of wildflowers that had been hidden among the weeds all my life until then, that nobody knew were there, especially me.

Chapter 11: Ann

Until I was thirteen years old I called her Mama. It's hard to call her that now. I can't say it. I can write it, but even then I flinch. It hurts to remember her now, but I do, even after decades of trying to forget. What I remember about her now is broken into bits and pieces. Some of it I have hidden from myself, and some of what should have been there, just never was.

When I was thirteen my life was altered completely, as if by some unexplainable act of God. From that winter day forward, everything in my life was changed miraculously and permanently. Suddenly I had a new mother who wanted me, one who was willing and able to earnestly love me. She was a more wonderful mother than I ever could have imagined in my wildest dreams, if I were capable of such dreams, which I utterly, absolutely, was not.

Ann was the woman who gave birth to me, we had the same blood, but there can be no shadow of a doubt that my real Mother, who would love and nurture me from that day forward for as long as she lived, who taught me the best about life and inspired me to seek it, was Helen.

Most of what I know now about Ann's life I never knew until the letters she wrote to me in the last years before she died. I didn't know till then that from her early childhood, she had been left behind, repeatedly abandoned both physically and emotionally by all the family she ever knew. She didn't complain about it. She didn't talk about it. I don't think anyone ever knew, until I asked and she confessed, in those last letters.

Ann was a kind and gentle person, that's all she was. As

a young girl she'd had dreams like any young girl does, but no real opportunities to seek them. She married a handsome sailor, my brother and I were born, and her life was set and sealed.

She was a good and decent woman who lost herself in a life she didn't know she chose, because she never knew she had choices. She took whatever came to her in life, and tried to make the best of it. She did what a good woman did in those days, she gave her life to her man. She never learned how to ask for anything for herself. That wasn't her fault, it was just what life had taught her when she was very young. The mistakes she made were classic ones many other women of her time made, and even I would make too. But the one that crippled her life and cost her absolutely everything was the addiction to alcohol, for which she would be held in disgrace. Nobody knew then, that an addiction was a illness, not an unforgivable sin.

I never knew my birthmother's name until after she died. She had been called Annabelle until she started high school, and then for the rest of her life, she called herself Ann. Her real name, unknown to almost everyone who ever knew her, I learned from the birth certificate the County Clerk Recorder's office sent to me along with some other old papers when she died. It was Amanda.

She'd had one close childhood friend, Millie, whose mother ran a boarding house in Greensboro. Annabelle was left there for weeks or months at a time while her mother, my Granny, was on a case as a traveling home healthcare nurse, what in those days was called a "Practical-Nurse." It was home-nursing and light cooking and housekeeping. On Ann's birth certificate, her mother's occupation was listed as "housekeeper." Annabelle and Millie were playmates as kids and best friends as young women. They both loved books and dreamed of becoming writers. They lost touch with each other when Millie went on to college, then ran into each other again years later in Washington D.C. in their twenties. I saw an old black and white photo of them, and I still remember it. The two of them are striding down a city sidewalk together, swinging along, arm in arm. In the snapshot they are bold and confident, very good-looking young women with bright carefree smiles. Ann is slender but very nicely endowed, a "sweater girl," with billowing, bouncing, shoulder-length strawberry blonde hair. They are both wearing slim skirts and snug sweaters. Blonde and brunette, classic American girls looking for life and adventure. They both wanted to be writers, and they both fell in love with sailors.

When Ann met George, they were in their early twenties and he was in the Navy. He must have looked very dashing in his dress-blues: the classic bell-bottom pants, wide-collar Midshipman's blouse, red scarf-tie and jaunty sailor-cap. That was the U.S. Navy's uniform in 1937. In another tiny snapshot, he is young and lean, with intense dark Greek eyes, "the strong silent type" that was the style of leading-men in movies of the time. For him, it was not an affectation, it was a shyness and reserve that was his true nature.

Ann fell hard for him, and he fell in love with her too. He wrote a poem about her that called her "a knockout," and spoke of how amazing it was that "a girl like that" could love him. What Ann did next, someday I would do also at about the same age. She handed over her life, all of it, to the man she loved.

There's no wedding picture. Maybe they had a civil ceremony at City Hall like so many servicemen did, long on passion and short on money. After his tour of duty ended, they had a son. Those must have been happy years for them. Then two years later, things got more complicated when her mother had a severe stroke, and I was born. Both events happened within a few weeks of each other.

We were happy in North Carolina, where we lived till I was four and Tommy was six. Then Mama and Daddy decided to go West to look for a better life. We left North Carolina headed for California and got as far as Texas.

More than once in my life, Mama told me, "Whatever you do with your life, don't be a waitress," and she said it with a barely-concealed regret. "You're on your feet all day; it's hard work, and you've gotta keep on smiling and be nice to people no matter how ugly they treat you. They act like they own you. Don't let people own you, Vickie. Do something else. Do something you want to do, if you can, but don't be a waitress."

Ann was a waitress all her life, right up to the day she died. As far as I know, she never was anything else. She did all she could to keep food on the table at home for us, until a chain of events began the slow-motion collapse of her life that would finally leave her at rock bottom, alone.

I know almost nothing about her life after I left the haunted house. I only know that she did finally pull herself up out of alcoholism, without family or help, a thing that very few people are able to do. It took years, but she did it, She led a clean and sober life from then on. I didn't know then, how heroic that achievement was.

There must have been good times when she and Daddy were young and in love. There were happy times for all of us in Greensboro, and in Texas when we lived at Colombia Avenue and Beacon Street. I remember those times and cherish them. The other times, the times that were not good, I shoved them away into a deep dark place in the most remote corner of my mind, and made myself forget them on purpose.

What I remember about her in the first years of my life is mostly foggy at the edges, but some things are clear and sharp. There was one day I remember perfectly. I was very small, maybe three years old in Greensboro. She had gotten a part-time job as a rookie reporter at the small local newspaper. I remember how happy she was, it was her dream-job and she was thrilled. I can see her, even now.

She is twirling around in the living-room, wearing a special outfit, a tailored dark-gray pinstriped suit. It has a flared skirt and a matching jacket that fits her slim waist. She has a shoulder-strap briefcase bag. Her hair is flowing down, golden, and bouncing off the suit's wide shoulders that were the style back then. She looks beautiful; she is so happy, like a girl in a magazine picture.

I guess she had to give it up to stay at home with my brother and me, or maybe Granny got sick again, I don't know. All I know is, she had that one wonderful day, and that was the end of her writing career.

My memories of her are faded like old photographs. She was there, but never very close. Across the table, across the room somewhere, with Tommy. I was with Granny, and we were happy enough with each other's company.

All I know about Ann's life before she married is mostly second-hand. Some of it I learned from her girlhood friend Millie. Decades later I tracked her down and talked with her on the phone. Millie did become a writer, and at 92 was still razor-sharp and working on a new book.

Millie told me what she remembered about her best

friend when they were little girls, and when they met again at twenty-something in D.C. Now after a lifetime, she wanted to know the rest of Ann's story, what had happened after they both married their sailors and lost touch with each other. I couldn't tell her anything happy, so I didn't say. When I asked her what Ann was like back then, she said what she remembered most was "She was very understanding."

When she was young, my birthmother was beautiful and brave. As a kid she was a tomboy who loved horses and books. What I know about her youth I learned only in the last years of her life, from the letters we wrote to each other. Our relationship was poignant and incomplete, but in those letters she answered some of the questions I had wondered about all my life.

Neither of my parents had finished high school. Ann dropped out to help at home just as her mother and grandmother had done. George dropped out and lied about his age to join the Navy when he was seventeen, and went to sea as his father had done. But as an adult, he studied at night to earn a GED high school equivalency diploma when he was almost forty. Ann never did.

More than anything else, she was kind. I never saw her be anything else except once, which was done in defense of her mother. At heart, she was gentle, she was soft, and she was vulnerable. She worked hard. She carried the weight for other people. She didn't want to, but it just seemed to fall on her shoulders and so she just carried it the best she could, until she couldn't anymore. She was loyal to her mother, her employers and friends, and I believe she was well-respected and loved by most people who knew her.

There are parts of my childhood that I have pushed into

darkness and can't remember even glimpses of. Months or years that are simply blank spaces. Maybe it's because for children sometimes there are things that are so painful that the mind in its mercy simply wipes them from the slate.

But even now, once in a while for no reason at all, old ghosts rise up, and suddenly they're here in the room with me. They just appear, uncalled, especially in the morning just after I wake up and I'm not quite conscious yet.

Today unexpectedly I thought of her, and *she was here.* As I stumbled to the kitchen to start the coffee, I heard the word inside my head, the way Mama used to say it in her soft Kentucky drawl: *"Cawfey."* I heard her clearly, as if she were in the room, and my thoughts flew away to Beacon and Columbia Street.

It's an ordinary Saturday morning and I am nine years old. When I wake up, I can smell the thick rich aroma of the coffee, and hear it burbling-up into the little glass thing in the top of the percolator pot. Mama and Daddy are talking quietly at the kitchen table, with coffee and cigarettes.

These are good times. Mama and Daddy smile at each other at breakfast. She has a day job at Mr. Joe Yee's Chinese and American Restaurant. We live at the corner of Columbia Avenue and Beacon Street. I am in third grade, and I walk to school and home again every day with my best friends Vivian and her spunky little sister Dimi.

Then I remembered the light silvery sound of Mama's laughter.

It's a breathy kind of laugh, soft and fluttery like her hair, which is fine and soft and golden with a touch of strawberry color. She is pretty, young and happy, laughing, drinking up life, cup after cup.

The memory seeps back like water from a hidden well, and I can see her. It hurts me to see her. For a splinter of a moment I remember, then I quickly close the remembering.

Decades ago I buried my pain deep and determined, so it couldn't hurt me anymore, so it couldn't reopen the torn places in my life that were left by the mother I never really had, who in so many ways never had a mother either. I regret that I didn't know her when I was a child, and I was unable to share myself with her as a daughter after I was grown. If we'd ever had a chance, we didn't know how to take it. When I separated from her at age thirteen, that possibility had ended, and it would never come back.

When Daddy and Helen got married they went to court to get custody of my brother and me, and a whole new life began for all of us. It was a Godsend for Tommy and me; it saved our lives, and it was a beautiful new beginning for Daddy. But it left Ann tragically alone, unable to work, with a broken wrist from the fall that happened when she was drunk or drugged, coming home from spending the night with a girlfriend "to make Daddy jealous."

When my father filed for custody, the lawyer made a case that Ann was an alcoholic and an unfit mother, that she had neglected and abandoned her children. It was true, but it was also true that we all had abandoned her too, even more than she had abandoned us, more than her mother, my beloved Granny had abandoned her so many times, when she was so young. There was plenty of guilt to go around.

Ann had never asked for much, so she got even less. She never knew how to ask for what she wanted in life, so I didn't either. She couldn't teach me what she never knew, and so it would take me half a lifetime to learn.

Sometimes now I wake up in the middle of the night

and can't go back to sleep. I get up and have a glass of milk. When I was very small in North Carolina, some nights I was fussy and couldn't sleep. Mama would bring me a glass of milk with chunks of white bread broken up into it. I ate the milky bread with a spoon and then I drank the milk. She did care for me then, even with everything else, Granny's stroke and Tommy's demands. She had to take care of two small children, a bedridden mother, and a husband. She did all she could for me, I know she did.

When I was twelve and my brother was fourteen, her marriage was falling apart. Then the haunted house, and the drinking got so bad she couldn't even take care of herself, that was why she couldn't take care of us. She needed somebody to take care of her too, and she didn't have that. Tommy and I had no way to help her except just to take care of ourselves so things wouldn't be so hard for her, and we did that. I think we both felt helpless and sad for her because we knew she was unhappy, but we couldn't change that. By then, all of us were drowning. Each of us did whatever we could to stay afloat, to survive. Not knowing where the tide was taking us and afraid to know, we lost each other.

Sometimes in dreams I return to East Side Avenue, the strange little upstairs-downstairs house where everything began to end.

I walk through the silent empty rooms again, and they seem perfectly real. The same peculiar wallpapers, and the same lumpy linoleum floors. The same loneliness that seeps through the walls and invisibly into the heart.

The places and the people are like scenes in a film, with close-ups and wide shots. The hot tar sheen of city streets glaring in sunlight, the blazing heat of noonday that burns your skin and you can smell it burning. The surprising patches of unexpected joy like the orange tiger-lilies growing wild and absurdly beautiful in the alley behind the garbage cans.

Inside the house, once again I am drifting through the dim airless rooms and the quietness of the small close personal spaces, like Mama's bedroom. Her old vanity dresser is still here, with its streaked and cloudy mirror, and the little pile of quarters on the corner of it, her tips from the night before, where she has dumped out her pockets, shucked off her waitress uniform and stumbled into bed without turning on the light, so bone-weary that she didn't want to have to speak or force a smile for another living soul. She just wanted desperately to sleep.

I stand again in the stillness and the hazy golden light of late afternoon. I see the old pink chenille bedspread and the cluttered dresser top, and I can feel her presence, as real as if she has just left the room a moment ago, and there is a lingering sense of her still in it. As if she has just stepped out to the drugstore down the street to get a pack of cigarettes, and she will be right back.

Chapter 12: Austin

"These are the best years of your lives," Professor Lester said at our college orientation at the University of Texas. He was right. Except for the sniper in the bell tower on the Quad and the shock of the assassination of JFK, these would be my happiest years ever.

College was the first giant-step of growing up. We all left our childhood and its limitations behind us and stepped out, free. We took the leap into a wide new world that was utterly unlike anything we had known before and we threw ourselves right into the tides of it.

We believed in everything. We celebrated our days, the sad ones as much as the happy ones. We were artists and poets and scientists and journalists, brilliant yet-to-become geniuses, and there was hardly any doubt in our minds. Best of all, we had an unlimited supply of tomorrows. We all put on the face of confidence, made new friends, and gathered together in flocks and clans like the unsure fledglings we really were. I joined the kinship of one of the most passionate of clans. I was an art student.

In those days, we were immortal. We were explorers, fearlessly naïve and foolishly bold, swept along together toward unseen destinies, ready or not. When things went wrong we wept our lovely young tears. When things went right, we reveled in the rightness of life itself. Whatever appeared in front of us, blind to the outcome we jumped right in. We were the Beautiful People of the 1960s.

I lived in Scottish Rite Dormitory, an elegant old four-story mansion of a building on the edge of the campus with a legacy of blooming magnolia trees all across its broad green lawn. The other dorms had cafeterias, but we had formal sit-down meals served by handsome young waiters. Their jobs didn't pay much and changed hands every semester, but to be an SRD waiter was a coveted bragging point for fraternity men. They and most other college men were eager to date SRD girls; we were considered prime catches. To live there, you had to be the daughter of a Mason, so it was assumed that our Daddies were rich. Some weren't of course; some just worked hard, like mine.

Through the first year and a half, college life was carefree, until I ran out of money. I had worked for a year in a fileclerk job Mother got for me at State Farm Insurance and saved up for college, but even though Mother sneaked a little more into my checking account when she could, at mid-term of my second year I had to move out of the dorm.

I was incredibly lucky to get a room to rent off-campus in an old Victorian house at 1609 Colorado Street, living on the second floor with three other girl students. My room at the corner of the house had two tall windows that opened onto lush pecan trees. I made magenta-purple curtains by dyeing some old cotton bedsheets Mother sent to me for that purpose. (Mother never wasted anything). They were always swept open, even at night, because nobody was going to look in, and even if they did, they would only see me at my desk, studying. My windows and my world were wide open, my life was benign and safe.

Renee, my ex-roommate at the dorm, helped me get a summer job where she worked at Kodak film-processing plant in Dallas where both our families lived. Kodak used extra help summers and Christmas season when people took the most color pictures and home movies. Everything was on film then, and had to be developed, printed, and packaged by hand. It was production-line work, skilled and repetitious, but it paid well. The graveyard shift paid most. Only the best workers, usually old-timers not the seasonal kids, could get that shift. Renee was on the graveyard shift. That summer my friend Peggy worked there too, and all three of us would work he night shift there Christmas vacations and summers for rest of our way through college.

The surge and flow of college life soon dissolved away my high school shyness. At the University of Texas, the boy-to-girl ratio was four to one, and I had droves of boyfriends at my heels like puppies. I could choose the ones I would allow to take me to dinner or a concert or a movie. At fraternity parties we danced to the Beach Boys and Buddy Holly and Roy Orbison, Bo Diddley and Fats Domino.

In memory the Austin days are bright and simple, like overexposed photographs whose brilliant light obliterates details. The seasons blurred together. September was still summer and waist-high sun-bleached grass rustled in the hot breeze in the vacant lot next to our house. Winter in Austin was brown and gray, occasionally rainy, and mostly mild. We all went out to the football games and cheered for our team, the U.T. Longhorns. I screamed, "Hook 'em horns!" though I had no idea what was happening down there on the field.

At midterm exams, art majors had few written tests, just Art History and a few Liberal Arts Degree required courses. For art courses a jury of instructors reviewed our paintings and drawings to determine our grades for the semester. Then almost before we knew it, it was spring again and the campus exploded with bluebonnets, blooming acacias, and billowy cottonwood trees. By May, summer was back, and the leaves of the trees were dusty gray-green leather things that clapped together like cardboard in the dry wind. Afternoons were too sultry to do much except take naps or go to the lake. When twilight cooled down a little, the air came alive with insects. All through the nights, mosquitos whined in the darkness. We slapped ourselves awake trying to kill them. Outside the open windows, feeble breezes wandered, and crickets and cicadas kept up their relentless madrigals that sang us back into a fretful sleep.

The first time I met Neil and Jim, we were all in the same art history class. One day the two of them were having a spirited debate about contemporary abstract artists in the courtyard of the Architecture building at class break. I was not really listening. I was watching them, observing how both of them played this game.

Neil seemed a quiet, pensive young man, maybe a little bit introverted. *Hmm. Interesting.* Jim was just the opposite, impulsive and agitated. He paced back and forth as he spoke and gestured frenetically with his hands. He was almost theatrically intense. I was amused by that. Neil was soft-spoken, serious and thoughtful as he responded, which I found attractive. Neil was good-looking in a brooding Teutonic sort of way. I liked that too. He was an artist, but he was also a varsity tennis player.

Their conversation was a debate about the merits of some abstract expressionist painters on the West Coast, the super-stars of a new style called Action Painting. As he spoke, Jim was constantly moving, never still, and there was fire in his eyes. Each time he raised his voice, his arms flew up too. I remember what he was saying because at the time, it sounded shocking to me. "Anybody can just masturbate a canvas and call it art!" he said, with far too much passion for the lovely autumn afternoon.

I wanted to get to know Neil, and though I didn't have any particular interest in Jim, I knew that he was a friend of Neil's, so a few days later when Jim invited me to a party at Neil's place, I went.

They both lived off-campus, Neil in a tiny odd house on the edge of a parking lot by a small clump of mesquite trees. Jim lived in the basement of a house where his friends Tony and Gilbert lived upstairs. That winter Tony and Gilbert's kitchen was a hangout for a small cadre of art students. Warmed by the open burners of the kitchen stove, we drank beer and talked about art while Gilbert doodled exquisite little pen and ink drawings. Amazing imaginary cities, beasts, and cartoon characters flowed from the tip of his Rapid-o-graph pen. Neil was often there, and since Jim lived downstairs, he usually was too.

I was dating mostly fraternity boys then and didn't have any intentions about Jim, but he seemed mildly interested in me. There was nothing said, we were just friends. I was dating a half-dozen guys casually, but I kind of had set my sights on Neil. I didn't tell anyone, but I was holding a special space for him.

Jim made me laugh. He was known for his witty sense of humor, though at times he could be moody and distant. The angry scrapper I had seen outside Art History class was one part of him, but there was a different part of him that was more hidden and vulnerable, even fragile. Most of all, Jim was passionately committed to his art.

In my plan to get closer to Neil, I was spending time around Jim too. There were group day-trips into the country to sketch the flat Texas farmlands, old weathered-wood barns, and fields of grazing cows. On these field trips we painted the vast flat rolling landscapes. Before I was aware of it, Jim had slipped into my heart by the back door.

Nothing was declared, or seemed to be needed by the social norms. We were art-friends. I had no interest in "going with" anybody, I was very much enjoying dating fraternity boys, being independent and sought-after. Need I say, I was a virgin, and I think that was true of all the girls I knew. I was becoming fond of Jim, had even spent some affectionate evenings with him, but I had not awakened yet to the sense of physical desire and wasn't even very curious about it. I loved my classes, my art, and my tribe of friends. There was an infinite road in front of me, and so much life all around me. I was in no hurry whatsoever to fall in love or any such thing.

We art students spent long afternoons in the oppressive heat and charcoal dust of life-drawing classes as we strained to capture the realness of the model's body, the livingness of it, and translate it into art. Standing at our large manilla drawing pads, with aching arms we carved the charcoal marks we hoped would miraculously make art. After three hours of this, we were more than ready for a cold beer.

Our favorite place to go was Scholtz's Beer Garden. We spent many relaxed lazy afternoons downing frosted mugs of ice cold beer at outdoor tables sticky with spilled beer and talked about art. At sundown, strings of lights that crisscrossed between the trees were lit, and there was music from a juke box.

For generations Scholz's Beer Garden had been the place where legislators from the State Capitol a few blocks away took breaks from all that arduous legislating, and unofficially, this was where the real deals were made.

It was also the place where the artists hung out. The legislators wore their suits and ties, and we wore the uniform that marked us as The Artists: light blue cotton chambray work shirts and wheat jeans. No serious artist wore slacks or a skirt. Blue jeans were acceptable, but wheat-jeans, an off-white cream color, were the style.

Weekends I was a coed again. I went to Frat parties or dates to small bars and clubs. It was illegal to sell hard liquor within one mile of the University campus, so college men took their dates to the roadside clubs just outside of town on the Austin Highway for drinking and dancing to jukeboxes or sometimes a live band.

One of the favorite places was a semi-forbidden black nightclub called Charlie's Playhouse. IDs were not checked carefully and it had a small crowded dance floor and live music. On Saturday nights the place was full of college kids. Charlie, a large amiable black man, greeted them at the door with a gleaming smile. A smart businessman, he must have made a good income on cover charges and beer from silly young white kids, many of them there for the thrill of doing something their parents would disapprove of. A few black couples came, mostly to set the atmosphere I think. Saturday nights the place was as white as Wonder Bread, but weeknights it came alive with locals from the neighborhood. The music rocked way hotter and it was a different place entirely. We usually went on week nights.

Another popular night-spot out on the Austin Highway was an old gas station that was converted into a bar called Threadgill's. Old man Threadgill was always there, in his Roy Rogers cowboy shirt and bolo tie. Every night was open-mike. There was no sign-up, just every so often the Juke box got turned off and anybody that wanted to sing or play could climb up on the bar and take the mike.

One night when my Theta Xi date and I were leaving Threadgill's to go to another bar, the New Orleans Club, I heard a voice that stopped me in my tracks and made the hair on my arms stand up. It was Janice Joplin. That was before her career as a rock singer, she was a folksinger. Joan Baez was the rising star who was about to discover Bob Dylan. Back then, Janice had a voice that was pure, clear, and spine-chillingly unforgettable. It was styled after Joan Baez, but about two octaves higher. It was incredible. I had never heard anything like it before, and I never would again. Later Janice would burn out her throat with whiskey and drugs and singing too loud in cheap noisy bars. It was that crippled raspy voice that would make her famous.

I enjoyed the boyfriends and other such foolishness, but I was a dedicated student, working toward a Bachelor of Fine Arts in painting, printmaking, and graphic arts. The old wooden barracks art building was always left unlocked during the day and early evening after classes, and anyone could come in and work. I spent countless contented hours in the graphics lab, printing my lithographs from local stones quarried up on the hill above the art building or printing my copperplate etchings

I loved etching best. The lab had a beautiful old hand-cranked etching press with a solid steel plate press-bed and a five foot high cast-iron wheel that you turned to move the press-bed with the etching plate through the press. This printed the etching onto heavy watercolor paper, pre-soaked and damp to receive the impression and the ink from the etching plate.

Most students used zinc plates, much cheaper than copper, but for drypoint, the most sensitive and subtle of etchings, I used pure copper plates, polished to a perfect sheen. The carbon-steel scribing tool cut cleanly into the yielding flesh of the soft metal in the most sensual way, and made each line complex and expressive. No acid-etched line could approach the grace and subtlety of the drypoint line in copper. It was like something alive. And while you could pull a large number of prints from an acid-etched plate, the number of prints from a drypoint was limited because the surface was vulnerable. The burred edges that made the lines so soft and dark, wore down and gradually flattened from the pressure of each pass through the printing press, so that the later prints lost some of the detail and freshness. Only the first few prints had the full beauty and subtlety of the line.

Oh, the sweet thrill of pulling the first print from the plate, peeling back the thick damp paper and seeing the image for the first time, crisp black and white, seeing it born.

Evenings I walked home from the art building through humid air that felt like wading waist-deep through warm water. After a day's work, I was peaceful and happy. I loved my life and hardly knew it; I took it all for granted. I lived as if there could never be anything else but this. Creating, discovering. An artist was a wonderful thing to be.

Although I could choose among boyfriends like seashells on the beach, I was in no hurry. I was only interested in someone really exceptional. He had to be someone stronger than me, and he had to be smarter and finer. The Knight in Shining Armor thing was the social standard. Men were assumed to be superior to women, even though reality often conflicted with that. But every girl knew that if we had to be owned by one, we wanted the best one we could get. For now of course, I was only window-shopping.

Jim was intelligent, talented, and dedicated to his art. He had a charismatic personality, brash and outspoken, which I interpreted as strength. Sometimes he tried to look serious and brooding like Neil, but his features were too fine-boned and soft. At twenty-one he could have passed for sixteen.

When I'd only known him a little while, he grew a mustache. All the male art students were doing it. But after the fad faded, he kept his. I guess he thought it made him look older. I thought it made him look like a used-car salesman, but it was part of his "image" so I accepted it.

Jim had never said much about his family, I only knew that his father had been a lovable alcoholic and his mother a loyal and loving wife and devoted mom. He told me once that his father had committed suicide by jumping out a window when Jim was sixteen years old. "I was just getting to know him..." Jim said, and he never spoke of it again. That was enough for me to know that this must have been an abandonment he could not bear, a wound that had not healed. Years later when he got drunk enough, his agony came back, fresh and raw as open flesh.

Jim was a double Aries the fire sign, both sun and moon. There was an explosive intensity about him, I'd known it the first time I saw him. On the outside he was full of energy and action, absurdly brave like a Bantam rooster. On the inside though, he was kindhearted, sensitive and vulnerable. He knew this, so he covered it up with flair and pride, humor and bravado. That's what a Texas man does.

It never occurred to me that I might love Jim. He was not a serious consideration. I was busy with other things, my art, my friends, and the Thanksgiving break coming up. I heard there was a party at Neil's place, and Jim would probably go, so I asked him for a ride.

I had never been much of a drinker. After a few beers I quietly fell asleep. A the party we were drinking cheap Chianti wine, which was trickier, less predictable. I wasn't into drinking anyway, but it was what my crowd did. I don't remember much about that night, it was like so many others. I remember all of us sitting around...

Music is playing and we are drinking and the guys are talking about art. I'm sitting next to Neil on the couch, and I'm already nodding off, feeling very relaxed and drowsy as I sink deeper into the couch cushions. I am bold enough to run my fingers playfully up the smooth skin of Neil's lower back, where no one can see. I rest my head on his shoulder and fall asleep.

The next thing I remember, I woke up and everyone was gone but Neil and me. I thought I was dreaming – but no, it was real.

Here I am, I thought, *right where I wanted to be. It must be very late. The room is chilly and his body is warm. My head is foggy, but one thing is clear, everyone else has left.*

We lay down on the couch together. We kissed, and kissed again. He was gentle, close and warm. His shirt was open and his skin was like silk. Except for that, we were fully dressed. I dozed in his arms. He was too much of a gentleman to take advantage of anything more, and so, wrapped up together we both fell asleep.

In the morning when Neil's phone rang I woke up with a shock. It was the first day of Thanksgiving break and my ride to Dallas had come to my house to pick me up. When I wasn't there, my housemates had called Jim, and Jim called

Neil and told him they were looking for me. I rushed home, and managed to connect with my ride. With no time to talk to either Neil or Jim, I rode from Austin to Dallas lying down in the back seat, hung-over and sick as a dog.

After the four-day holiday I came back to school. Jim didn't call for nearly a week. When he did, I met with him at his place, to talk. I told him the truth, that Neil and I had just held each other and fallen asleep. I wasn't sure what this would mean to him or to our undefined relationship. We sat together in the dark in silence. I felt so much guilt and remorse that I could hardly speak. My thoughts tumbled in circles.

I should not have to feel guilty; I haven't done anything wrong. I had arrived at the party with Jim, but not as a date, and Jim had left me there. If he thought I was some kind of a date, he should have waked me up, but he didn't. He left me there alone with Neil.

Confused and conflicted, my mind jammed its gears at the question: *Did Jim think I was "his girl?"*

It wasn't clear. Nothing had been said. If he did think that, then I would have been a terrible person to flirt with Neil. If not, I had the right to be with anyone I wanted, and from the beginning, it was Neil I wanted.

Up until then, I didn't know that I had begun to care for Jim more than I intended to. He was a good person and a good friend. I wanted him to take me back.

Neil was the reason I'd gone out with Jim in the first place, but neither of them knew that. To further complicate things, I hadn't known how close their friendship was. I didn't know that they'd grown up together since grade-school in Nebraska. I had spent one night alone with Neil, and now Jim was sullen, hurt and withdrawn. Though it could be argued that it was not a date, if he thought it was, he should not have left me there, and yet, Jim held it over me as an unforgivable debt to him. And so did I.

He shouldn't have. And I shouldn't have.

I had not committed any sin or crime to be punished for. He should not have blamed me, and I should not have blamed myself, but I did. I had awakened that morning feeling alarmed and guilty, as if I had done something wrong, even though I had not. When Jim reacted as if I had, I fell right back into the role I had hated so much as a child: the quiet, compliant, obedient, good little girl.

As we sat there together in the dark of Jim's room, tears poured silently down my face. I promised him that if only he would take me back, I would do anything to make it up to him. I didn't know then what I was promising.

Chapter 13: Port Arthur

The art building was an old converted army barracks building at the far end of campus. A wandering stream called Waller Creek ran past it bordered by a grove of small trees, just enough for shade. It was quiet and dim there. You could sit by the creek between classes and imagine you were in a forest instead of a crowded college campus.

On the street side at the back door of the graphics lab, a grassy hillside rose sharply like a living wall till it ended at a paved parking lot. Starting early in spring and lasting into the fall, that hillside was covered with wild poppies in extravagant abundance. Blood-red to scarlet, their silken petals fluttered in the breeze like the whirling skirts of gypsy-girl dancers, and the wantonness of them seemed to shout for joy. Every time I walked past them my heart beat faster and a tight little ache gripped my throat, as if my soul might leap out of my body and rush to dance with the poppies in this celebration of life.

Painting and drawing instructors often used bunches of them for still-life subjects, and as we worked, the poppies bgan to wilt. Within the hours of a class they would die, while out on the hillside, the others still danced in warm winds and glorious life. The poppies became a symbol to me of a special kind of courage, the courage to live free. For when they were cut and taken, they refused to live.

Everybody liked Jim. His energy was magnetic. He was always surrounded by bright creative people, and when I was with him, I was too. He had friends on the staff of the University humor magazine The Texas Ranger, and one of them, Gilbert, would someday be internationally known as a comic artist for the characters he created for the Ranger at his kitchen table in Austin: Wonder Warthog, Fat Freddie's Cat, and the Furry Freak Brothers.

But the one person Jim called his best friend was Steve, whom he looked up to like an older brother and spoke of almost reverently. Steve had graduated and was pursuing his painting career and living with his girlfriend in Port Arthur. One weekend we drove down to visit him.

Port Arthur was a grim little town. There was not much to do there, and all afternoon, Jim and Steve drank beer and talked endlessly about the good old days, and smoked pack after pack of cigarettes. Steve's girlfriend Linda just drank and smoked. I sipped lukewarm beer and waited for the trip to be over.

Finally it got very late, the Jack Paar show had ended, the TV screen was a test pattern, and there was nothing left to say. Everybody went to bed. Steve and Linda slept in a back bedroom, Jim bedded down in an armchair in another room, and I slept in the living room on the couch.

Falling asleep groggy with alcohol, I heard foghorns far off in the sultry darkness. At first I thought, *What a strange dream.* Port Arthur was just a name to me. Like Fort Worth wasn't a real fort, I hadn't realized that Port Arthur was a actually a port, with ships, until I heard the foghorns in the thick heat of the night, calling mournfully to each other like lost souls.

Port Arthur was a shipping port on the Gulf of Mexico with a population of about 40,000. It would have been a completely forgettable experience, except that it was where I lost my virginity in the middle of the night with the foghorns moaning somewhere far out there in the dark.

It must have been three or four in the morning. I was asleep when Jim crept into my bed. When I felt the pain and woke up, it was too late to stop him. It wasn't romantic or passionate, and by the time I came awake, it was almost over.

I don't think he said anything at all. He got up and went back to his chair and back to sleep. I lay there shocked. There was nothing I could do about it, it was done. With no magic moment, no words of love from prince charming, I was no longer a virgin.

The next day there was only the strange ache in the torn place. Jim told me he had heard Steve and Linda having sex in the back room and that was why, extremely drunk, he had come stumbling into the room where I was sound asleep, and crept into my bed. This was apparently intended as some sort of apology.

I didn't know what was happening until it happened. I didn't want it to happen, but whatever my excuses, it had happened, and it changed me in some way that I did not understand. Somehow it had branded me, and after that, I belonged to him. Nothing was really said, but from that time on, I felt somehow bound to him.

For the rest of my life, I never drank that much again. I never went back to Port Arthur Texas and never will, but I never forgot it either. I made a mistake there that changed the course of my life.

At the end of May Austin was as hot as August. It was the week of final exams and artwork juries for classes and when those were finished, the grades would be determined and the school year would be over. Jim would be leaving for New Haven Connecticut where his first semester at

Yale's graduate School of Art and Architecture would begin in the fall.

The time that was left, Jim and I spent together. We stayed close. Evenings we sat on a blanket in the back yard of the house on Colorado Street where I lived, trying to catch whatever breeze there might be. When the school year ended he left, and even though I hadn't meant to fall in love with him, I felt the loss as if a part of myself had been borrowed and not returned. We write letters to each other every week and make lots of long-distance calls. There was really nothing to say, but we missed each other.

Jim was not exactly a prize. His thin angular body was not athletic, his face was too young-looking and too soft. But what he may have lacked in looks, he made up for in wit. He was charming and articulate, a lightning-rod of personality, He was a clever comic and a great storyteller. Even when he was serious, then too he seemed to stand out in a crowd, quietly intense.

He was tall and lanky but he had gotten his height late, not until he was twenty. I think even after he was six-foot-one, he never really felt big enough. He had been an only child raised by a single mother after his father's suicide when he was sixteen. Maybe that was why he needed so many people around him, like outriggers on a canoe, to help him balance himself.

I went home and through the summer we wrote letters. School started again in September and his life got busy with all sorts of new things and people. At midterm semester break he came back to Texas.

We talked about it, and decided to get married. There was no engagement ring, just the mutual decision. The proposal, such as it was, happened at the edge of a lake. I don't remember where. Neither of us was ready for marriage but we couldn't bear being apart and we thought that this was the only way we could be together.

I reasoned logically enough that with him I would have an exciting life among creative people. it never occurred to me that I might be left out of the circle, or that I could have found an exciting life anyway, on my own. In those days I lived on the outside of myself, directed by what other people wanted me to be. I didn't realize yet that I mattered too, that I myself was a legitimate factor in my own life. How could I not know that? Nobody had ever told me.

I never really wanted to get married. I don't think Jim did either, but when he started graduate school at Yale, he was on the East Coast and I was still in Texas. We missed each other so much and our long-distance phone bills were so expensive, marriage seemed to make some sort of sense. I could move to Connecticut and we would be together. Just "living together" would have been more practical, but it was 1963, we were good kids, and good kids like us didn't do things like that.

The wedding would be at Christmas vacation. I would come home to Dallas and Jim would come back from New Haven. After the wedding we would have a few days together, then each of us would go back to our separate schools in separate cities 1,600 miles apart. I would finish the rest of the semester, then I would leave school one semester short of graduating and move to New Haven.

Meanwhile Mother and Julia, Vivian's mother who had crafted my prom dress, were busy fitting my wedding dress, planning the flowers and the reception, reserving the church, and all the multitude of details for the wedding.

Everything seemed to be rushing forward very fast. I had a bad feeling in the pit of my stomach, I was ambivalent and apprehensive, but I struggled to ignore it and plunged ahead anyway. Jim and I both had wanted a very small wedding, but Mother wanted to make it wonderful for me. When the wedding day came, even with Mother's perfect plans in place, everything that possibly could go wrong, did.

For one thing, it snowed. It never snows in Dallas, except about once every forty years, but it snowed on my wedding day. The guests were coming by car and nobody was used to driving in snow. They had to drive slowly, slipping and sliding on the ice of streets and freeways. The wedding guests were late, and so was the wedding.

The wedding had been scheduled for the afternoon at three o'clock. My dress was street-length with a fingertip-length veil. But since the ceremony was delayed by traffic, it was after four, an evening wedding, so it properly should have been a long dress. No matter, we went ahead.

I barely remember the wedding itself, except Daddy walking me down the aisle. I looked over at him and there were tears in his beautiful brown eyes. I panicked. I knew I would fall apart if I saw my Daddy cry, so I started saying something silly to cheer him up. I had wanted to look graceful walking down the aisle with a swanlike elegance. Instead I went nervously laughing with a silly look on my face. As Jim and I stood before the minister to say our vows, Jim's voice failed and faded to barely a squeak, so I lowered mine too. Nobody in the church heard either of us say "I do."

After the ceremony, Jim and I were the first ones to arrive back at my family's house for the reception. Jim got out of the car. The driver-side door was closest to the house, so instead of opening my passenger door and walking around the car in the snow, I reached over and grasped the driver's side doorframe to help myself slide across the car seat to get out the the driver door. You could do that in Jim's old pre-bucket-seat Ford. Jim was reaching into the rear door to get our coats from the back seat. He saw me slide over, and in his hurry to help me out of the car in a gentlemanly way, he quickly slammed the rear door, smashing my finger in it.

With a look of horror at my shout, Jim realized what he had done, and reopened the car door to free my finger. He stood there helplessly with a stricken look on his suddenly ashen face. As I stepped out of the car, my finger dripped a few bright red drops of blood onto the flawless white of the new snow. I held my hand out in front of me so it wouldn't bleed onto my pretty little white satin shoes. A gust of wind caught my veil and swept it forward in a tangle over my face, tearing my hair where it was pinned. No one else had arrived at the house yet except us. In that moment I realized I didn't have a house key.

We both stood there. Jim's face looked desperate and completely unnerved. Trying to comprehend it, and struck dumb with disbelief, I thought, *This can't be happening*.

A car pulled up behind us, the first people to arrive for the reception. It wasn't Mother and Daddy or anyone with a key to the door. Of all the people it might have been, it was our old neighbors from Stigall Street, Mr. and Mrs. Murphy and their son Roland, the young man everybody thought I would marry but I didn't.

At this point my memory screen goes blank. We must have stood there together very awkwardly until Mother and Daddy came and opened the house door.

As soon as we got inside, somebody gave me some pills for pain. Daddy devised a bandage that stopped the bleeding and drew the two sides of the split fingertip together and secured them. He chipped some ice and wrapped it in a dishtowel to make an ice pack for me. Mother brought me some other pills, I think they were a mild tranquilizer. I hadn't eaten anything since breakfast, so the combination of stress, an empty stomach, and medications took effect. I don't remember much pain after that. In fact, I don't remember very much of anything after that, except smiling at all those people in our living room milling around, smiling at me. The reception flew by in a haze. I had to walk carefully, a sort of shuffle, because I couldn't feel my feet. I was smiling for a long time at one pretty girl in a red velvet dress who was talking to me. In my drugged haze I wondered who she was, and then I realized it was my sister Mary. I don't remember the rest except what I saw later in the wedding pictures. In every picture of the reception, I'm holding the dishtowel ice-pack in my hand.

Somehow Mother got me changed into my going-away suit. People threw rice in tiny sheer-net bundles tied with ribbons as Jim and I came out the front door. We drove off to the Marriott hotel where Jim's mom had reserved a lavish room for our one-night honeymoon.

In the lobby we were dazzled by a two-story open foyer with an enormous cut-crystal chandelier hung in the center of its vast space, and a curved stairway swept majestically upward on one side of it. Everything was bright, glittering, splendid. The room was decorated in plum-purple and beige with a wall of mirrors near the bed. Later a lot of sex happened there which, drugged and oblivious, I was only vaguely aware of.

At 4:00 a.m. we both woke up severely hungry. Neither of us had eaten anything all day except the wedding cake, which I didn't remember either. Jim went out into the hallway and found a Coke machine. We shared a can of Coca-Cola and finally went back to sleep. My smashed finger was throbbing urgently. I fell asleep anyway. That's all I remember about my honeymoon.

Whatever her shortfalls in life may have been, my birth-mother Ann was braver than I knew. I'd seen her only twice since I was thirteen. Now, after all she had been through – addiction, loss, abandonment and shame, she came to my wedding. Mother had sent her an invitation out of respect, and of course, no one expected her to come. But she came. That must have taken unimaginable courage.

The last time I'd seen her, I was sixteen and she was a recovering alcoholic. I had no idea what that meant at the time. Mother had arranged for me to visit her and urged me to go, so I spent one day with her, and overnight. She had been sober, going to AA meetings. She was nervous seeing me, and the experience was painfully awkward for us both.

Now after all those vacant years, here she was. She was wearing a royal blue dress, white gloves, and a little fur shawl, all very tasteful. She may have borrowed it all, but she looked better than I had ever seen her. Her hair was nicely done, with a little blue hat, and she wore a touch of makeup. She probably couldn't afford it, but she had come by taxi to North Dallas where I lived with my new family.

I didn't see her at the wedding, everything was moving so fast and I was swept along with it. But she came to the reception at our house.

Regrettably in my drugged state, I didn't give her much

attention. Even under the best of circumstances I would not have known what to say to her. The wedding, the crowd, the pain of my smashed finger and the effect of too many medications different people had given me had set my head spinning. I couldn't even focus my vision very well.

Mother insisted on taking a picture of Jim and me and Ann together. What that must have meant to Ann, I cannot imagine– all of this– to see Daddy again, to see his new wife, to see me in my wedding dress, and to see her grown son after nearly ten years. Yet she looked completely composed, and prettier than I had remembered her. She seemed a rock of strength and courage, as far as I could tell through my Darvon blur.

Ann's presence was quiet and unobtrusive. Only our family and closest friends knew who she was, and Mother welcomed her warmly as any other guest. Nobody else knew what a heroic act it was for her to come there, into a crowd of strangers. It was something I recognized as uncommonly brave. I don't think I could have done such a thing myself, not the person I was then. And yet this was very like some intrepid and improbable things I too would do later on in my life. There must have been a streak of bravery in both of us, and I still believe it came from Granny's Kentucky blood.

Mother, as always, was beautiful and gracious and kind. No corsage had been ordered for Ann, since no one had expected her to come. Mother took off her white orchid corsage, gave it to Ann, and pinned it on for her.

Mother was the classiest woman I have ever known.

Chapter 14: New Haven

After the Christmas wedding we spent a few days at Jim's mom's apartment in San Antonio, then Jim went back to New Haven and I went back to Austin to finish the rest of the semester.

Every week he wrote me sweet letters about school and the new friends he met. Once he sent me a tiny sycamore leaf that blew in his window as he wrote. I counted the days, and as soon as the semester ended I went home to Dallas, packed my bags, and left for Connecticut.

I got on the train wearing a nice little traveling suit and my warmest Texas coat, which wasn't nearly warm enough. The ticket was coach, an old Burlington train. The seats were hard and cold. I shivered the whole two days, and when I finally arrived in New Haven, the charming old city greeted me with dirty snow and bone-chilling cold. It was after midnight when Jim picked me up at the New Haven Station.

The first night of our new life together was not the romantic love-story reunion I had imagined. In fact it was awkward and almost depressing. There was some rather uninspired weary sex, and then he hogged all the covers and I shivered through the rest of the night. My first winter on the East Coast would be cold and wet, hostile and mean. It would be like living on the moon, and I didn't know how. I had to learn.

Jim's aunt Norma lived in Manhattan. She was terrific, warm and fun and very cosmopolitan. She had found the apartment at 55 Norton Street for Jim when he came out that summer to prepare for graduate school in the fall. It was a small third-floor walk-up in an old wood-frame house on the corner of Chapel and Norton. The first floor was a Public Accountant's office with an entrance from the street. It had a business glass door, a small foyer with the accountant's door on one side and a stair of four or five steps on the other. At the turn of the steps where they went out of sight, they narrowed abruptly to only about 30 inches wide and climbed steeply to apartments on the second and third floors. At the top of the last flight of stairs were two small apartments in the dormers of the roof. One was ours. The rent was $90 a month, which seems incredibly cheap now, but in 1964, it was hard for us to manage.

That first week, Jim got a postcard from Neil. He had joined the Marines. Nobody would ever have expected that. Neil had been the quiet one, the most introverted one of us. He had been athletic but his art was sensitive and subtle. He was also a musician. Now a Marine? Maybe he wanted to prove something to himself, or maybe he was trying to find himself among all the different selves he had inside him.

I had to find a job as soon as possible but I was just out of school with no degree and no experience except a file-clerk job at State Farm Insurance and the summer job at Kodak. Wives of Jim's new friends helped me find leads, but weeks of job-hunting passed without success. The more I slogged through the slushy streets, the lower my hopes descended. On the radio, the Mamas and the Papas were singing *California Dreamin'* and I could not even imagine that dream. Paul Simon sang: *I am a rock; I am an Island.*

I was willing to take almost anything, and finally there was a want-ad for a clerical job at Southern New England Telephone Company. I applied. They gave me a battery of tests, long strings of numbers to look at for a few seconds, memorize, and then write down. I passed the tests and got the job. After that, I was bringing home $52 a week, and as far as I knew, that was what we had to live on.

Jim kept the checkbook. That was the one piece of advice my mother-in law had given me, one day when I'd said, "I guess we'll open a joint checking account." She said "No, Jim should take charge of financial matters; he needs to learn how to be more responsible with money." That was a mistake. He never did learn to be responsible with money.

The telephone company job was mechanical and deadly dull. I collected five-layer service repair orders endlessly rolling off teleprinters, separated them, alphabetized them, collated five copies of each service order into five stacks, sorted them, then delivered them to the proper departments, desks, and file drawers in the sprawling office. I worked in the Directory department, which filled the entire fourth floor of the Southern New England Telephone Company on George Street. Four managers and forty girls compiled, produced, and maintained both the White Pages and the Yellow Pages. We sat all day hunched over our desks, shuffling papers. By mid-morning my neck and shoulders ached and burned.

The other girls were nice enough, but I was an oddity there. Behind my back they called me "the beatnik." I wore my dark hair long with Cher bangs. They all had cute short stylish hairdos and trendy Carnaby Street clothes.

Eventually a few had the courage or the kindness to befriend me. My best friends, the ones I could talk to were Carol Lawson and Sylvia Vaughn. Carol was my age, a great person with a lively bright open mind. She was undecided between two boyfriends and she had a pet iguana in her apartment that lived under her kitchen table. I liked her right away, she was different from the rest.

Sylvia trained me as a new employee. She was forty-something, really my closest friend, the oldest of "the girls" in the department and the only black woman on the floor. Sylvia was a gift. She had a genuine warmth about her, a wisdom about life, and a great sense of humor. That was what got me through. I don't know what she ever saw in me. I think she saw something like a stray puppy that called out to be befriended.

The first East Coast winter was a test of survival. North Carolina had been cold and Texas could have its ice storms, but Connecticut had a wet, penetrating cold that found its way into your shoes, inside your coat collar and down the back of your neck. It seeped through your clothes, all the way through to your bones.

Our apartment was an attic, right under the roof. Whatever the weather was, snow or ice or rain, we were right next to it. By the time the feeble heat came all the way up from the furnace in the basement, the vents had already given out what little warmth they had to the first two floors and brought us only a slight cool draft next to the bedroom wall. A thick wad of ice formed on the inside of the window and stayed for months. When it finally melted in spring, water dripped onto the ugly brown carpet beside the bed.

Spring continued cold and wet but when summer finally came, it wasn't so bad. Days were sunny and sometimes even hot. I loved being warm; it reminded me of home.

Outside the bedroom window was a huge Sycamore tree

almost as tall as the house. From the tiny bedroom window I could look down onto its lush canopy of leaves, each one tender green and flawless. They fluttered and waved to me like a sea of little hands.

I went to work every day at the Telephone Company, and like most of the other married students' wives, I came home to another full day's work of cooking, housework, and laundry. Jim went to New York on weekends, and in the beginning sometimes he took me with him. I saw wonderful art in museums, paintings by the masters of Impressionism, Post-Impressionism, and Modern art. There were magnificent paintings I had only seen pictures of in art books, works of genius and magic by Matisse, Monet, Van Gogh, Giacometti, Picasso. Jim's friend Brice who lived in New York took us to uptown galleries like the Leo Castelli Gallery where I saw paintings by pop artists Andy Warhol and Roy Lichtenstein and sculptures by John Marin. I marveled at it all.

But the best thing about New York was Jim's fabulous aunt Norma. She was a fashion model and lived in a big apartment building at 30 East 9th Street, between Cooper Union and Greenwich Village. She was not the pretzel-stick haute couture type of model, she modeled tasteful clothes for Town and Country and other upscale magazines. She was petite for a high-fashion model, only five-foot-eight, with short brown hair and beautiful hazel eyes that smiled.

Norma always put us up at her apartment whenever we came to New York. Without her the city would have been utterly bewildering. She was a real New Yorker, cheerfully at ease in the middle of the busy flow and flurry of it all.

We could walk from her apartment to the small clubs in the Village like the Purple Onion and the 9th Circle where we saw Nina Simone, Dizzy Gillespie and other jazz musicians. We could only have one beer for the evening because we were so broke. After Jim drank his, he drank the rest of mine. We held onto the bottles to keep the waiters at bay. We didn't fool them, they gave us haughty looks, but they let us stay.

We were shocked at the cost of everything, compared to Texas. When we were out and about we survived mostly on Nedick's hot dogs and orange-drinks. Evenings, Norma and one of her boyfriends took us all to some of her favorite restaurants. If it hadn't been for Norma, we might have starved in Manhattan.

One time She took us to Chinatown by taxi and we stood in line for more than an hour to get into a special restaurant. The place was gloriously alive, every inch of it swarming with happy people, elbow to elbow. Everybody was talking loud, and everything around us constantly moving like a pot boiling over. Waiters rushing among tables, everything brightly colored, spinning, sparkling with strange exotic life, and the food was delicious beyond description.

Another time, Norma's boyfriend Barney took us in his Lincoln Town Car through a tunnel to a fabulous restaurant in New Jersey. We ate and ate, and every table had bottles of seltzer so you could burp and eat more. I had my first experience of chopped liver with schmaltz. Incredible.

At heart, Jim's aunt Norma was still a farm girl from Nebraska, she didn't believe in wasting food. When she went to fancy uptown restaurants she always got doggie bags and brought home steak and lobster for her little poodle, Bijou. When we were in New York, she brought it home for us.

Jim's Mom Wilma in Texas was a daughter-in-law's dream. She kept in close touch with us and she was so thoughtful and considerate of our pride when we were so broke. She and I were about the same size, so she bought cute "Villager" skirts and tops for herself, washed them a few times so they wouldn't look too new, and sent them to me pretending they were hand-me-downs she was tired of.

There's a picture of Jim and me together at Norma's apartment in New York that first year. At twenty-two years old, we both look about sixteen. There's another small snapshot taken by Kaare and Pat, one of the other art students at Yale and his wife who befriended us. Kaare was 100% Norwegian and Pat was 100% American; her family could actually trace its lineage all the way back to the Mayflower. They took us skiing, with patched together old equipment Pat's grandfather and grandmother had used when they were our age. We went to a place in Middletown Connecticut to ski at night when it was cheaper and not crowded. I fell on my butt about a hundred times on the bunny hill and had a marvelous time.

Pat's grandfather had been an avid camper, skier, and snowshoe hiker in his youth, and he had built a large log-cabin on a piece of land he owned in upstate Connecticut. Kaare and Pat took us there on a camping trip. It was a two-day trip by car and boat to get there. The first night we stayed in a little wooden shack at the edge of the Connecticut River, built specifically at the halfway point of the journey for that purpose. I spent the night miserably not-sleeping on a hard wooden bench, Jim and I both in one sleeping bag that was not big enough for two people. In a snapshot the next morning, all of us are having breakfast at a table outdoors. My long dark hair is in two braids and I have no makeup on. I look exactly like an Ojibwa girl.

When we got to the grandfather's cabin it was deep in the heart of a beautiful fairy-tale forest of ancestral trees, majestic giants so tall you couldn't see the tops of them. Thin wire-like shafts of sunlight filtered down through them like the strings of a golden harp. The forest floor was covered with delicate feathery-leafed ferns and a spongy carpet of living moss. It was a magical place. That night Jim and I slept in sleeping bags in a tiny alcove under the roof on a bed of straw like an eagle's nest. The nights were cold but the days were magnificent. It was like traveling into another world, but only for a few unforgettable days.

Jim's friend Brice was in love with The City the way other artists might be in love with Paris or Rome. He worked as a guard at the Jewish Museum and knew all the galleries and museums in New York. He took Jim and me to places that were not on the tourist maps, like The Cloisters. We took a subway and then the 5th Avenue bus all the way to 193rd Street. I nodded in and out of consciousness with a blazing headache and a terrible case of the flu.

The Cloisters is a museum of Medieval art built from parts of several ancient abbeys, with ceilings supported by stone arches and columns from the Abbey of Saint-Guilhem-le-Desert, built in the year 804 A.D. It had been rebuilt from monasteries and cloister walkways brought from Europe, stone by stone, and reassembled here.

Beneath vaulted ceilings we walked among paintings and wood-carvings, tapestries, illuminated manuscripts, and stained-glass windows, most of them dated from 1000 A.D. to about 1500.

The sacredness of this place feels hauntingly present, as if the souls who once walked these halls are watching from overhead. Our voices echo off stone walls as if the words are passing through some other ancient space and time. I am astonished to realize that because of art, some of the far distant past is still living, here in the present, even though it was created by hands that now have been dust for hundreds of years.

When I first met Jim he had been an abstract painter, like Brice. Willem DeKooning, Jackson Pollock and Franz Kline were the successful artists of the several abstract genres of the time. Some abstract styles were geometric images like Brice's work, and several were a non-figurative style called action-painting, built up with wild strokes and splashes. By 1963, one of the early action-painters, Richard Diebenkorn, had developed another kind of abstraction with figures, and a flat, color-rich style which he called "color-field landscapes."

In the art program at the university of Texas, Jim had been an action painter, one of the MTs, art-speak for "major talent." He had been awarded a summer scholarship at Yale that was a life-changing experience for him. In his senior year at U.T. he applied for admission to the Yale graduate School of Art and Architecture, and he was accepted. The application had required students to submit photo slides of their work, and at that time, most of the slides Jim sent probably were abstract paintings.

I didn't know when the change had come for Jim, or why, but by the time he got to New Haven that fall, his interest had made a complete turn-around, from action-painting to figure painting and still-life. He was working in a style that was figurative, personal, and very different from the East-Coast-abstract trend at Yale.

Jim studied the works of the Post-Impressionist painter Paul Cézanne, an artist who experimented with space in a paradoxical way no one else had done. Cézanne was a favorite of mine too. Jim also liked an obscure painter named Giorgio Morandi who had been popular in the 1930's for moody minimalist still-lifes that had an odd sense of mystery.

Jim also admired another painter of that period called Balthus, who painted pre-teen girls in sexually tantalizing poses in dimly-lit interiors, which often included a lurking cat. The effect was dreamlike, enigmatic, sensual, and a bit disturbing. In the Modern period of art, Balthus had been called by art critics an "anti-modernist," but after his death, he would be called "a figurative master in an age of abstraction." Now, in the 1960s, he was rather obscure.

Like these artists, Jim was a rebel mutineer. He began to paint figures, portraits, and still-lifes of unusual objects. My friend Sylvia at the telephone company told me about a neighborhood flea market on Legion Avenue every Sunday. We went there and found all sorts of treasures for Jim to paint: beautiful old wooden hand-tools, ceramic jars and vases, and metal utensils with functions that were unknown now, but whose shapes were poetic and mysterious.

At Yale graduate school the environment was highly competitive and extremely demanding. Jim was as talented in his new style as he had been in abstract painting, but it was not the popular mode of most of the other students. His vision was different, and I knew he felt an undercurrent of reserve, even disdain, from other students and even some professors for his style of painting. He was often frustrated and discouraged. He raged every day, and I tried to be supportive.

This new life was not as happy for me as I had hoped it would be either. For both of us, the challenges were formidable. At school he was well-liked by fellow students but seen as a sort of outsider, different. At the telephone company, I was too.

For me there was joyless work and no hope of any pursuit of my art. For Jim there were days in art classes and evenings with other art students at a little pub near school. After my workdays I came home to housework, almost always profoundly tired. I longed for rest and sleep, but I had signed-on for this life, I had taken a vow and made a promise without knowing what I was promising myself to.

I came to dread the nights most of all. Every night I was expected to surrender to "my wifely duties," no matter how tired I was, no matter how late it was when he came home from drinking with his friends. He woke me up for it. Whether I was sick or well, he collected his dues. It wasn't romantic; it was a habit for him. Maybe not even so much for pleasure as simply a way to appease his frustrations over his struggles to succeed at school. Maybe that was a way he could feel in control of something. All I knew was, it was not anything about love.

I had never known lovemaking, never had the pleasure of that with the man I married. In the beginning there were glimmers of it, and biology made my body want something it could not know. But in marriage I got only the mechanics of the act, without the good feelings, and without the love. By law, sex without consent is rape, but rape is too strong a word. Rape is an act of violence, this was neither violent nor passionate, it was mechanical and impersonal.

There were times I pleaded for just one night off, but he would not let it go. He kept on coaxing and then when the lights went out, he took what he needed, and that was the way it was. Each time I asked myself, *How could someone who was otherwise a kind gentle person be so unfeeling and unaware?*

Each time, I felt used and ashamed. I held my breath and strained to not cry out in pain. When he was done, I turned my face to the wall and began the work of forgetting again. I was not a person to him, and I knew it. I was a thing that he owned, that he had the right to use however he wished. I accepted this because, foolish or not, I had committed my life to him. I had left my old life to come to this hostile place, and now he was all I had.

I'd been taught that a good and decent wife never says no to her husband's needs. I was a fool, but I was a good and decent wife. I had friends at work, but women didn't talk about things like that. We smiled and pretended everything was fine. My family was half a continent away and I would never have told them anyhow, for the shame of it. I never did tell them. I never told anyone until now.

It would be easy, so many years later, to make him look like a villain. He was not. He was thoughtless, but never intentionally cruel. He was a talented artist, of that there was no question. When he was sober, he had a brilliant sense of humor that was warm and heartfelt. He could make me laugh, and I had not laughed a lot in my life. On a good day, he could make me love him just for that. He had heartbreaking flaws, but he also had a wide-eyed honest faith in life and art, even though he had been wounded by both. I understood that.

I was deeply disappointed, but I followed the rules I was taught in childhood: Be good and be quiet. At twenty-one I was not very smart. I'd been taught not to stand up for myself, so I didn't. An honest mistake. I didn't know I had the right to matter in marriage. No one ever told me that.

I didn't blame Jim for his ignorance or my own. It was what it was. It was a hard lesson, but there was nothing else for me to do but learn it, and it had to be learned before I could move on. So I learned it and learned it and learned it.

Jim loved New York, but the crush and hurry of the city overwhelmed me with anxiety. In the daytime it swarmed like an anthill on amphetamines, every street an endless surge of pushing, bustling bodies. After the rush hour, nothing really stopped rushing. The density thinned out in some places later into the night, but not Downtown.

The city became a carnival of neon colors, and Jim's friend Brice loved to go out into Manhattan at night. He went around humming and half-singing the popular song by Petula Clark, "*I know a place, where the music is fine and the lights are always low. I know a place where we can go.*" That wasn't where we went this night though. I can't tell you where we went, because I didn't know.

It's very late. The streets are dark and empty except for a few slow-moving creatures that must have once been people, but who now seem to be wandering souls, drifting, waiting around to be released from whatever it was they have– not a life, but something dreadfully else.

I remember that night, the cold, the ache and sting of it, and how the jagged-edged winds tore at my hair and flung ice needles in my face.

The streets are desolate, dim even in the streetlights, barren except for the dark figures hunched in doorways. Yesterday's crumpled newspapers, shoved by gusts of wind, stumble along the sidewalks like crippled old ghosts with nowhere to go but no place to stay either.

Brice was taking Jim and me to see some friends. It was supposed to be a party. Brice knew lots of people; he was a New Yorker. We knew nobody but Brice, we were fresh from another world: college and Austin Texas.

We took a subway, then a bus, then we walked several blocks through gray canyons of concrete and cinderblock. When we reached the destination, it was a bleak building like all the others we had passed.

At the door, Brice rang the apartment number. There was no answer. He rang a second time and we waited, blowing white clouds of breath in the freezing dark air. He rang a third time, and once again we waited.

A muffled answer blurred through the voice tube:

"Who is it?"

"It's Brice," he said. There was a long silence.

A loud buzzer sounded and a steel click deep in the heavy brass door signaled the momentary release of the lock. Brice pushed open the door quickly and we went in.

We climbed sIx flights of stairs to the third floor. I was grateful there was no elevator to jerk and shudder with frightening uncertainty like they do in these old buildings. There were no bums sleeping in the stairwells, only a faint smell of urine. Brice found the apartment, and knocked. It was 2:15 AM.

The door opened and a pale woman stood there in a flannel nightgown with faded pink flowers and coffee stains. She looked about forty, not pretty, but handsome in a gaunt Medieval-saint sort of way. Later I would learn she was twenty-something like us. With a limp gesture she motioned us to come in. She seemed unsteady on her feet, which were bare. With effort she raised her heavy eyelids to speak. I couldn't quite make out her words.

"This is Sheila" Brice said to us. We smiled awkwardly. She didn't smile back.

"How're you?" she asked Brice. She glanced toward Jim and me

"I'm good." He said. "Where's Dan?"

"I dunno. He split couple-a weeks ago, maybe a month. He'll come back. He always does."

She offered us some wine, Fior de California, a popular vintage for musicians and artists like us. It tasted like vinegar but it was only two-fifty a liter.

Conversation was minimal. We sat on a dusty Goodwill Store braided rug. There was no furniture except some couch cushions on the floor and a colorless balding wall-to-wall carpet. The apartment was cold; we didn't take off our coats. Sheila didn't seem to notice the cold, even though she was wearing only the nightgown.

"Were you asleep?" Brice asked apologetically.

"No. I was working on a song. Wanna hear it?"

"Sure." he said.

She disappeared for a few minutes and returned with a scarred and battered old Harmony guitar. She sat down cross-legged on the rug and began to play. As she sang, her body rocked gently back and forth. Her voice was pleasant, a haunting folksinger style. She finished the song and didn't offer another.

Brice said, "That's nice. Really." She mumbled a reply. We sat in silence for what seemed like a long time, then Brice got up. We got up too. We thanked the woman for the wine and shuffled to the door.

"Take it easy" she said to him. She still had said nothing to us. We went back down the stairs without talking and out onto the street again. "She wasn't feeling so good," Brice said, "but they're really great people."

Outside a misting rain drifted down, with fine droplets swimming in the halos of the streetlights. We walked back to the bus stop. We waited a long time for the bus.

Jim went to New York as often as he could. At first sometimes I went too. But after a few months of the job, the housework, and never enough sleep, my health and spirit both slowed down like an unwound clock. I was too tired to enjoy the trips, the toll was too high, so I have fewer happy memories than there might have been. Those few weekends in the City were all I had of "the artist's life" that Jim and I had both dreamed of in college. I was a wife, not an artist. Now Jim had grad school at Yale and other artists to talk to, and I had the Telephone Company.

But those times in the galleries were unforgettable. I stood before some of the greatest artworks in the world, like the Van Gogh exhibition at the Guggenheim. The stroll down the spiral was a diary of his life, the paintings and the order of them, from oldest to newest, first to last. The first ones are dark and depressed, but the last ones pure rapture, brilliant and glorious orgasmic ecstasies of color. They said that Vincent was losing his mind, and he was never very happy, but his soul must have been soaring.

At the Metropolitan I loved the Impressionists and Post-Impressionists best. Seeing them up close was absolutely transcendent. I had seen all of them in art history books, they were as familiar as old friends, but now they were not photographs, they were the real thing.

There was one huge panel from a series, Monet's Water Lilies, on loan from its permanent home in Giverny, France, where he had lived and worked in the last years of his life. It must have been forty feet wide and twelve feet tall, and it seemed to draw all of the light and air of the immense gallery room into itself in some miraculous, numinous, magical, impossible way. I stood there numb, thunderstruck with awe.

Art history would someday call him "the father of Impressionism" but in his young days he was out of step with the mainstream of art. What was unique about Monet's work was that he didn't paint pictures of *things;* instead he sought to paint *the light that fell upon them*. He didn't paint in the style of the academics and recognized artists, he was doing something else. The critics were outraged. "These are just sketches!" they said. "This is not art!" That was in the late 1890's but today his paintings are in museums all over the world. Reproductions of them are in tens of thousands of Art History books.

This Waterlilies panel was part of an immense series that fit together to create a continuous scene of a glittering summer-lit pond of water lilies in his garden at Giverny. It filled the entire opposite wall of the gallery room, and the moment I entered, I stopped astonished, like Alice when she stepped through the looking-glass. I was swept at once into a living garden, transfixed, and overwhelmed by the intense realness of it.

The depth and liquidness of the water is almost surreal, the weight and floating-ness of the lily pads, like islands on the reflective surface. The sunlight is hypnotic, flooding everything.

For a moment I almost heard the buzzing of dragonflies.

I'd never seen anything like this. It seemed to be moving, shimmering with light. *It was alive.* I had to see, up close, how human hands could have worked this miracle.

But as I walked closer, it all began to disassemble and change, transforming itself into a vast expanse of beautiful, wildly random patches of rich colors, dabs and streaks and splashes of paint-strokes. As I came very near, the water lilies, the sunlit garden pond, and the whole world as we know it, *disappeared.*

I stood open-mouthed, shocked, bewildered. Then I turned and walked back to the other end of the room, and when I looked again from there, *it had all returned.*

A chill started at the crown of my head flowed down through my body like a slow electric current all the way to my feet. In that instant, I realized something. *You have to look at the whole of a thing.*

You have to look at the whole of the thing to see the order of it, the truth of it. The parts and pieces, like the strokes and lines and colors, can be beautiful in themselves, but if they are true, they create a larger image, a larger truth. And more than that, they can create a thing like this - a living entity that seems to move and breathe and give off a light of its own.

When my consciousness returned to the room, there was another student artist standing to my left. His focus on the painting was just as intense as mine, and he was completely unaware of me. Unembarrassed tears trailed down his smooth young face. Both of us stood there without a word, without a sound, for a long time, looking at the painting, drowning in it, soaking up as much of it as we could. Both of us knew we might never be in the presence of anything like this again.

In the entry foyer of the Museum of Modern Art, near the gift shop Matisse's Dancers romped gaily across a large canvas, a vision of joy that I could see, but I had no way to feel. I loved the colors and the movement of it, and I thought, *I'd like to paint something like that...* and maybe I could have, if things had been different.

I remember the museum's small courtyard, the little outdoor cafe on a rainy gray afternoon, and sitting beneath fragile sapling trees with bare branches as delicate as a silverpoint drawing, glistening with diamonds of rain. The chilly hope of spring, still fragile in the air, the little white ironwork tables, and raindrops in my coffee.

Chapter 15: Us

He had his share of personal faults, but as an artist, Jim was a beautiful spirit. He was viscerally passionate about his art. Because I was an artist too, I knew he was truly gifted. His work was deeply earnest, but it was no longer flashy and stylish the way it had been when he was a brash young abstract action-painter, and now there would be dues to pay.

There's only one of his abstract paintings I remember, painted before I met him. At one semester break I'd gone with him to San Antonio to meet his mom, and he took me to meet his high school art teacher and mentor. That's where I saw it.

It was about five feet square and dramatically dominated her living room wall. The painting was alive with energy and movement, boldly splashed and spattered with many unexpected shades of white, small patches of browns, subtle dashes of greens, and glimmers of other colors. The brush-strokes were audacious, tempestuous, exciting. There was no recognizable object or image, yet there was the unmistakable message of a thawing winter landscape at the very edge of spring.

The painting was titled "The First Warm Day." In it I could see the melting snow, the first fragile green shoots of life renewing itself, and almost smell the spring mud. It was a splendid painting. I understood in an instant why the prestigious Yale graduate art school had given him the summer scholarship that would bring him to New Haven a year later, and ultimately change my life as well.

Jim never told me why he changed his style. I only knew that the decision was true to some inner directive, and he had followed his heart instead of his ego or practical mind. Honestly, I don't think Jim ever owned "a practical mind." He had the soul of an artist and the hidden tenderness, fervor, vulnerability, and rage of a latter-day Vincent Van Gogh. He obeyed his inner imperatives, and that was his downfall.

In my mind I can still see that painting, and the title is embedded in my heart forever. Every year when the first signs of spring begin to emerge again, I take notice, and quietly celebrate the first warm day.

I had married an alcoholic and didn't realize it. We all drank in college. Hot nights in Austin we drank cold beer and the boys got roaring drunk. That was normal. It never occurred to me that Jim might have an alcohol problem, and yet there were clues I should have seen and somehow I didn't. Jim didn't drink during the day, and he didn't hide bottles in odd places like my birthmother Ann had done, but when we went to events where there was alcohol, he drank till his whole personality changed. He became uncharacteristically loud, even verbally abusive. Jim had seen his father's alcoholism shatter his family, and yet he fell into the same trap himself. I married a man I thought I knew, but there was more of him beneath the surface that no one could see. I hadn't really known him at all, and he had not known me.

With the pressures of grad school, Jim was prone to outbreaks of explosive anger and frustration. He *raged* a lot, that was his primary coping skill.

But he also had a brilliant wit, an innate talent he must have developed when he was very young, to camouflage his fears and his feelings. Without it he was naked. When things got too painful to fend off with humor, he covered his vulnerability on the inside with rage on the outside. Any tender feelings like sorrow, disappointment, love– those were difficult for him to show, and impossible for him to speak. So instead he raged, broke things, or hit a wall with his fist, but even in the worst of his rages, he never hit me.

When he was hurt, he raged. When he was sad, he raged. When something happened that he could neither express nor contain, he raged. In the three years in New Haven, he raged almost every day. There was so much going on inside of him that had to get out of him somehow, so he shouted and smashed things, or hit the wall with his fist. and when it was over, he retreated silently inside himself. Later he made jokes about it, or simply forgot.

Jim had grad school, other artists, and intelligent creative friends. I had the telephone company. I was not an artist anymore and I had never been a star like them. At the rare school parties when we met other couples, Jim introduced me as "the wife." One of those times, another student's wife blurted out, "Does she have a name?"

"Oh... yeah," he stammered, "It's Vic." And he laughed, embarrassed. He didn't like Vickie, the name I was called when we met, and Victoria was too formal for him, so he called me Vic, a name that would stay with me for seven years before I remembered, that was not my name.

When I married Jim I left my home and my happy life to invest in someone else's dream, to be "the woman behind the man" as Texas tradition expected. I gave up my goals for his. I thought it would be only for a while, and then I could have a life and career too. I took a chance, I drew a card. When I didn't get what I wanted, I believed I had to take whatever I got. I accepted it because I had always been taught to "just take it." I couldn't think of going home to Texas, not after my parents had spent their savings to give me a wonderful wedding, and then Daddy and Mother with tearful smiles had sent me off to my new life. What could I tell them?

"He doesn't care about me as a person. I am only a thing that he owns. He owns my body and he owns my life. Nobody told me it would be like this. Before we were married, I was special to him, now I am nothing to him. I am so much less to him than his worn-out favorite old jeans that I keep on mending, and he goes "Thanks babe" and never even looks up when he says it."

How could I tell them that? I could not.

Because of Yale, New Haven was a focal point of creative genius. It was the beginning of the era of the Beatles and the Rolling Stones, but before I was even aware of them, I had the great privilege to hear the magnificently gifted musician of the sitar who soon would so profoundly influence the Beatles that they would introduce his music to a whole new audience in the Western World.

Sri Ravi Shankar was in the U.S. for a college concert tour. Someone on the Art School faculty had invited him to stay at their home during his New England series of concerts. A party was given for him, and Professors and students were invited. The elegant old Connecticut home was crowded with distinguished people and talented students, talking together about important things I knew nothing of. I felt anonymous among the intelligentsia and the bright sub-swarm of art and music students. I hardly spoke two sentences all evening.

The hosts served a chicken curry so hot that it was almost inedible, and yet so delicious that I kept trying even though it burned every inch of my mouth, my throat, and my stomach like a lava flow. It was authentic Indian curry, a thin broth over rice with a few recognizable chicken neck-bones, but most of the ingredients had dissolved completely into utter deliciousness in slow simmering, all day long, stirred and attended by a flurry of lovely dark-eyed ladies in bright colored saris printed with flowers and bordered with streaks of silver or gold.

Sri Ravi and two of his students sat down in a raised cushioned area at one end of the living room. The lights were dimmed, and a hush of respectful quiet fell over the throng of celebrants. Then, in absolute pin-drop silence, the miracle occurred. They began to play.

My eyes were locked on the circle of warm light where the musicians sat, and the rest of the darkened room blurred away. With the first notes of the sitar, I was stunned. This music was like no sound I had ever heard, an unearthly wail of beauty so tender, so exquisite, that I was immediately engulfed in it. Everything around me faded, dissolved, and disappeared.

Language has no words to convey the beauty and mystery of the sounds of the sitar. "Transcendent, spiritual, numinous," all fall far short of this throbbing, weeping, rejoicing music that overflows the senses so that the mind falls back in awe. Serpentine lines of melody and deep resonant humming of strings swept and murmured and pulsed through every cell of my body. I stood transfixed, submerged in the music.

Sri Ravi was a quiet, kind, gentle person, often teaching one-to-one, sharing his art which he passed on to his many students. Profoundly modest, he spoke only a few words that night, but he left me with a legacy and a lesson:

"Whatever the gifts we are given, we must use them with honesty and gratefulness, as best our human failings and strengths will allow." In that moment, a thought came to me. *I've been given some gifts, but I have failed to use them.* And I was ashamed.

In college I had discovered myself. I found out that I was a strong person with a good mind and some talent. I decided that whoever would share my life would have to be a strong man. He had to be stronger than me; that was the Texas tradition. Jim's assertive personality seemed strong in the beginning, but it was not. It was only his armor.

The rules of chivalry required women, especially wives, to be inferior, no exceptions. I tried and I succeeded, but I lost myself doing it. Like an awkwardly tall girl slouching to look shorter than her date, I found my spirit always inwardly slumping down.

Very little of what I got married for turned out to be there for me. An article in Time magazine stated it perfectly when It said: "The primary reason so many marriages fail is that the institution of marriage has been designed for one and one-half persons..."

The exciting creative artist's life, the companionship and friendship that Jim and I had in school, or I thought we did, had disappeared. I'd made my choice and commitment, and now I was trapped in it. Marriage was not what I had expected and it was far from what I wanted.

In my role as half a person, I was at times a showpiece, "the wife," but more often, a useful adjunct. The ideal personal servant, I took care of all his domestic needs, cooking, dishwashing, laundry, ironing, and picking up all the small messes he made, dropping things everywhere he went like a teenager littering a park with candy wrappers. I worked full-time at a meaningless job to support us.

I had wanted a partnership. I didn't get that. Instead I had taken on most of the responsibility with none of the authority and no access to any of the money. There was no closeness, little or no communication, and I was obligated to surrender my body for sex on demand 365 days a year with no options and no exceptions. After we got married, it was as if we became strangers, both of us taking on roles that didn't fit. He didn't know how to be a husband, and I didn't know how to be a wife.

I had not made a very good bargain for myself. I had given up my art and gone to work to support his– assuming this would be temporary. That was not a smart assumption.

I had spent my days at a telephone company desk, filing service orders for installations and repairs. My world was an ocean of gray steel desks, row on row like sad moored battleships with nowhere to go. In grad school, Jim had challenging classes and afterwards cheerful friends and frosty mugs of beer, the way I used to do too, only a year ago in Austin.

When I got off work, Jim picked me up. Sometimes he forgot or he was late. He always said "Sorry, babe." and gave me one of those heart-melting boyish grins that were supposed to make it all okay.

It wasn't okay, but I didn't say it. At home I cooked dinner and managed to stretch six chicken wings into enough for two people. It wasn't enough, but I made sure he got enough, and I took what was left. I was as much a mother as a wife, and he was like a child in many ways. I could not hate him for that. I could not blame him.

While I cooked, Jim watched Rocky and Bullwinkle cartoons on the little portable TV in the living room. When I called him to dinner, he brought the TV with him, put it on the kitchen table and watched it while he ate. If I asked about his day, he'd say "I've really got a lot on my mind tonight babe, I just need to relax." So I let him.

In the Cinderella story, the girl turns into a princess in the arms of her adoring prince, he takes care of her, and they are happy ever-after. I know that's a fantasy, but I want a little bit of that. I don't want to have to tell Jim that I matter, I want him to notice. And as foolish as this probably sounds now, I want him to cherish me.

After dinner he went back to the school studio to paint some more, then afterwards to the pub with his friends. I knew he would drink too much. I went to bed and couldn't sleep, afraid he would get into a fight or a car crash.

I am a miserable little housewife with a miserable little life completely predicated by my husband. He is the center of my existence. I have no center for myself, and so I have no self.

Out there in the world, life rolled on. Disco came and went, Motown music emerged, then the Beatles. John was my favorite, the poet, the thinker. They were barely boys, the same age as me, but they were being shaped by a period of discovery that would bring a worldwide opening of minds, for better or for worse, and a creative out-rushing of music and art. The Beatles blithely and innocently fell into the vanguard of all that. Swept along with it, they went from Liverpool to fame, to drugs, and finally to meditation.

I didn't go anywhere. Just the Telephone Company, the grocery store and the laundromat. The music on the radio was dreamlike, from another world than mine. The Mamas and the Papas sang *California Dreamin'* and Paul Simon sang *Hello silence my old friend...* The soul of me, if it was even still alive, was somewhere else, abandoned and alone.

Sometimes it feels like my soul is an astronaut, spacewalking outside the ship, floating at the end of that thin little lifeline which might break at any moment, and if it does, my spirit will drift helplessly into black endless space.

There were some times it felt as if my soul was a thing apart from me, connected only by the frailest thread, and at risk any moment of being irretrievably lost. I was seriously depressed and I knew it. I could no longer deny it to myself, though I still hid it from everyone else. There was so much about myself and my life that I could not understand, and I could not face.

One night I left the house without asking, without even telling Jim. I don't know why I did it. Maybe something he said, or something he should have done that again he didn't do, or didn't see, or just forgot, again. I don't know what possessed me; maybe I was trying to make him notice that I existed.

I just walked. It was long after dark and the wind was blustery and cold, blowing the first thin dust of snowfall off the sidewalks. The night sky was moonless indigo blue with pale yellow halos around the street lamps like the ones in a Van Gogh painting. I wandered the streets with no destination, feeling vaguely sad. My mind felt inert and empty. I watched the little white clouds of my breath in the cold air, appearing and fading away, appearing and fading away, and I felt the cold begin to seep through my clothes. It was all pointless of course; I knew there was no place for me to go.

In the yard of an apartment building, I found a long-dead hydrangea flower that was still on the bush. I broke it off by its brittle stem and looked at it in the lamplight. It was pale beige, perfectly preserved by the cold dry air. Its tiny petals were crisp and fragile as insect wings, and yet completely, flawlessly intact.

I walked all the way to the laundromat. It was empty. I stood outside and looked in through the sooty windows. Inside, the fluorescent light was greenish and surreal, like always.

Jim brings me here once a week. He piles the bags of dirty laundry into his car, drives me to the laundromat and drops me off. I do the washing, then I watch, hypnotized, while the dryers tumble it dry. I fold it while I wait for Jim to come back for me. Sometimes I wait a long time because he has gone to the tavern with the guys and forgotten me until he gets home and notices I'm not there. Then he remembers. He always apologizes and gives me a sheepish little-boy grin, and sometimes I mumble, "It's okay." But it isn't okay and there isn't any smile at my end of it.

Our first months in New Haven, he came with me a few times and helped fold the clothes like other couples did. Then I guess he decided there was no point in both of us sitting here as the washing machines sloshed back and forth, so he left, promising to come back to fold, but he never did. The custom became the drop-off and pickup only.

A big truck rumbled down the narrow street behind me and a gust of wind whipped the tail of my coat. I turned away from the laundromat window. It was getting colder and the night air stung my face. There was nothing more to do but go back to the apartment where at least it was warmer.

When I came back, Jim looked at me but said nothing. I put the frail skeletal dried flower into an empty vase. It needed nothing but air. It had a delicate beauty, even though it was only the shell of what it had once been. It carried a message for me that I didn't see yet, that my life was like that flower; it had form but no color. I existed but I was not alive.

Jim was impulsive with money. He didn't seem to have any practical sense of economy. He had access to the checking account and I didn't. I had no knowledge or control of our finances. I had no voice in how he spent the money even though I was the sole wage-earner of our income.

When spring came again, one day he brought home a bicycle for me, a shiny new Royce-Union 3-speed. I was surprised and baffled by the gift. He expected me to be thrilled, but I knew that it had cost my whole paycheck, and we could not afford it.

Jim had brought his bike from Texas, so that evening we went for a ride together with some friends, Ron and Maureen. It would have been fun if I had not been so dead-tired. There was just that one ride, then never again. Later I realized the reason for the gift was so that I could ride it to work every morning when the weather allowed, so he could sleep late and not have to get up and take me to work.

When the second summer finally came it was beautiful and warm, and when Jim was gone to New York I had time to rest. Evenings were long and the twilight lingered sweet and calm. I sat at the little third-floor window, looking down on the leaves of the Sycamore tree. My thoughts wandered.

The leaves are so perfect, lush and green. They look like a crowded throng of little children's hands, reaching up, making a lovely canopy. I could just step out the window and walk there, and the little hands would hold me up, and they would feel so cool and gentle on my bare feet...

I jolted out of my reverie with the realization that to do that, to step out onto the little hands, would be certain death. They would not hold me up, and I would plummet three floors to hard concrete. My skull and most of my bones would be shattered. When I caught myself having thoughts like these, brief escapes into semi-hallucination, it scared me.

There were other moments when I wondered if maybe I actually did not exist. *I wasn't sure.* I was uncertain enough that when I walked down the sidewalk, I took care not to walk too close to anyone, for fear they might pass right through me *and then I would know* that I didn't exist. These and other moments of ambivalence made me secretly fear that I might be very quietly, privately, losing my mind. I began to be aware that my soul wanted desperately to escape, and I feared it might be willing to abandon my body, to do it.

Another winter came, colder and wetter than the last. It didn't matter. All my days were the same on the outside, and whatever of myself I had left, I hid it on the inside. I started to write poetry in secret. I turned to the empty page when there was nowhere else to go. There I could tell the truth, and somehow that helped. I knew no one would ever see it, but still I had to tell it. Telling it released the pain a little, it rose and diffused and let me live another day. The first poems were certainly not literature, but they were windows into some truths I had hidden from myself and did not know until I saw them for the first time, on the page.

A the end of the second year, students sent out resumes and applications for teaching jobs or made arrangements to move to New York or the West Coast to begin careers as professional artists. Yale School of Art and Architecture, like all the East Coast Ivy League schools, guarded their reputation for excellence. Graduation standards for a Master's Degree were high and stringent. If any student's final jury of artwork was not deemed good enough to compete successfully in the Art World, he or she would not graduate, but would be allowed a third year to demonstrate the ability to have a professional career as a artist. If the works of the probational third year were still judged not good enough by the faculty jury, the student would be released from the program without a degree.

Jim was one of two students who the professors felt unsure of, and so at the end of our second year in New Haven, He did not graduate. It was still not over.

All Jim's friends graduated and went to New York or teaching jobs scattered across the country. Chuck got a Fulbright Scholarship to study in Bavaria. Always the joker, he said he applied because he wanted to ski. He was serious about his art, but he had a quirky sense of humor. For his passport picture, he shaved off his thick full head of hair, and traded his horn-rimmed glasses for vintage wire-rims. With his bushy beard he looked remarkably like Sigmund Freud, which we all found hilariously funny.

But for Jim there would be the embarrassment of a third year, more expense, more pressure, and the stigma of being left behind. That year he was quieter. He didn't go out drinking as much, and he got a part time job two days a week at the art school library. Jim would make it through the year and so would I.

It's the raw wet edge of our third spring. I have come to the little park, two blocks down on Chapel Street. I left the apartment and came here by myself without telling Jim. It's late afternoon and everything is washed with a pale watery sunlight so weak that it barely casts a thin shadow. The ground is frozen mud, bare of snow, and the first bitter-green needles of grass have pierced upward eagerly from the dark earth toward the light.

I can't remember why I went. I couldn't have known this brief hour would wake the first stirring of something in me that I couldn't name. Something was beginning in me, and something was ending.

That evening after Jim went back to school, a poem came. I titled it "Forsythia" for the spindly spring shrub that blooms earliest in spring and can survive in almost any climate. There was something about seeing it blooming there in the park in spite of everything, all by itself in a sea of mud.

> I only remember the forsythia
> in Edgewood Park,
> yellow stars on a dark brown stalk,
> the only color
> at the muddy end of winter.
> I went out for a walk and didn't come back
> for nearly an hour.
> Went without reason, went alone,
> I sat on the hillside
> numb with cold, and thought
> absolutely nothing,
> and felt
> absolutely nothing,
> except the faintest stirring.

Of what? Of hope?
Or just the forsythia?
When I came back, your face was white
as if in fear,
as if you knew something broke in me,
and we could not pretend
that I didn't matter,
any longer.
But I said nothing.
Your color returned.
You kept your pride
and the private fears you could not show me,
you dared not show me.
You kept your secrets and I kept mine,
and you never tried
to know me.

What are we, Jim? Say something. Say anything. Before it's too late, look at me just once. Look me in the face and see me. I'm right here; I've been right here for you all this time. I have loved you and followed you to this barren place.

Something shifted in me today, and something changed. I'm beginning to let us end, like you have let us end, I'm beginning to give up on us.

There isn't any us. There's just you over there in your life, and me over here in the shadows clinging to the edge of it. That's not enough. It never was enough, and the chance for any kind of Us is running out.

At the end of our third year, he graduated. He sent out resumes and got an offer for a teaching job at the Minneapolis Art Institute's College of Art and Design. We were moving to Minnesota, even though we weren't sure exactly where it was. We had to look it up on a map.

Jim's New Haven years had been hard, but mine had been hard too, and bleak. In New Haven, our life had been *his life*. The colorful life I had imagined for myself had turned out to be as gray as the old city and the frozen salty slush of its narrow streets. We would be leaving New Haven when summer came, and then my life might change.

Chapter 16: Minneapolis

I had wanted a partnership, closeness, and a loving kind of sex. I didn't get any of that. Instead I got soul-numbing hard work and loneliness, and three years of my life had passed by. But then Jim got a teaching job, and suddenly I had *time*.

It was summer. I spent most of the days drifting around the new apartment while Jim was out and about doing whatever he was doing. The apartment was modest but bigger than the attic in New Haven, and it was warm. It was the upstairs of a small duplex on a tree-lined street in an old Jewish neighborhood on Russell Avenue North, rented from the family that lived below.

I began reading Zen books. My mind was open but blank, and it absorbed the writings of Suzuki and Watts like a new blotter. Someone had given Jim *Zen and the Art of the Archer* and I read it. I burned incense, drank tea and did other things that seemed Zen-like. I sat in the Lotus position, closed my eyes and tried to meditate.

I wandered through the first weeks in a fog, but with a profound attitude of peace and rest. As my head began to clear, I found myself in a different place of mind. I began to take an objective look at my life, like a seagull flying over a landfill. Marriage, for Jim, was a pretty good deal. Not for me. I had left a happy creative life in college and handed over my future to his care and ownership. He had wasted the best of me, and I had let him.

Getting out of New Haven and the Telephone Company felt as if a window had opened and light was pouring in. At first it was blinding, but a sense of my self had begun to stir, returning like a ghost. Gradually, almost imperceptibly at first, it began to take on substance and life.

"You just need to find *your thing*." Jim said, and walked away. "You don't have a *thing*." Like he had his art and his teaching, his students, other instructors and friends.

"All you gotta do is find your thing."

I hadn't had a "thing" for more than 3 years, and didn't even know where to look for one.

In Minneapolis, the people were friendly and welcoming, so different from the East Coast lifestyle. Minnesotans were kind and outgoing. Jim's teaching job didn't officially start till September, but summer classes were open. Tuition was free for wives and families of faculty, and now Jim was faculty. *Faculty! What a beautiful word!* In a drawing class I met Susan who was also an artist, and we became friends. I introduced her to Jim and to Jim's new best-friend Joe, another just-graduated new teacher. Susan liked Joe, and before long we became a natural foursome.

Joe was a city-boy from Chicago and he was eager to go fishing in Minnesota's legendary 10,000 lakes. There were many small ones near Minneapolis, abundantly populated with crappie, (pronounced "croppy,") A small round flat fish like a sunfish, easy to catch and devilishly delicious battered and fried crisp and brown, skin and all. Minnesota also had other more challenging legendary game-fish that Joe had read about in Field & Stream magazine. Jim, even though not a fisherman, immediately got swept up in Joe's enthusiasm. They went out together and bought fishing gear: rods and reels, lures, tackle-boxes and tents, and Jim ran up a large credit card debt.

Since I had worked to support us for three years in New Haven, when Jim completed his Master's degree and got his first job, the unspoken agreement was that he would become the breadwinner. I guess he forgot that his first paycheck from the school would not be coming until September, and now he had splurged a whole lot of money that we didn't have. I would have to go back to work.

With regret bordering on despair, I put in my application at the Minneapolis Telephone Company. I was experienced in their special codes and systems, so that would be my best chance for getting a job quickly. When I went to the job interview, it felt like surrendering to some unjust cosmic law enforcement and going back to jail. I cried a little bit on the bus. At the door of the personnel office, I wiped my face and went in.

I got a job, Customer Service Rep, with a two-week paid training class that met every day in a conference room in the old Kresge Building on the Nicollet Mall downtown. Erected in the 1920's as an elaborately stylish art-deco showcase, it had four floors, a fancy lobby with pink-veined marble floors and a sweeping curved staircase, roped off now with a small chain and placard: "closed, please use elevator." The building must have been splendid in its prime, now it housed only the Kresge dime-store and lunch counter at street level, and upstairs pigeon-hole offices and small businesses. A Timex watch repair, an Electrolysis hair removal, a shoe repair shop, Nellie's Alterations, an optometrist, two dentists, and a chiropractor. Most of the rest of the building had stood empty for years.

It was less than a week into the training when Jim got a phone call from his mom.

"Norma is in the hospital," she told him. I couldn't hear

what she said, but I saw Jim's face collapse as he listened.

"What hospital? he demanded. What happened?"

"She's here with me, in Dallas..." Wilma said. Jim's mom was Norma's older sister and they were very close. "and she won't be going back to New York."

When Jim hung up the phone, I waited for him to speak. His face was white as plaster.

"Norma has lymph cancer."

In shock and disbelief, I felt my knees go weak. I sat down at the kitchen table.

"It can't be true," I said in a whisper. "It can't be true!" *No, no please God, not Norma! Not beautiful joyful Aunt Norma. It can't be true. Please God don't let it be true.*

But it was true.

The doctors said her prognosis was "grave," the term they use when it's the worst possible. The cancer was rapid-spreading and terminal. "She might have as long as a few months, or at best, less than a year." The news abruptly crumpled the scaffolding of everything I had ever believed in about life.

I couldn't comprehend it, and yet I couldn't force it out of my thoughts. I loved her so much. She had been the one bright light through my lonely bleak years in New Haven. She was our fabulous "Auntie Mame," She was as young at heart as we were in years. If anyone should have had the longest, happiest life ever, it should have been Norma. She was only thirty-nine.

The next day when I went back to the small airless room of the Telephone Company training class, I couldn't keep my mind on the training material. The instructor's voice faded away, droning in he background, and I couldn't stop thinking about Norma. In the middle of the class I don't know what happened to me, but something welled-up from inside of me and suddenly I lost control and I started to cry. Surprised and embarrassed, I tried to hide it, but everyone saw. Tears were pouring down my face.

The instructor, a sweet older man, looked helplessly distraught. He took me outside to the hallway and asked me gently if I was all right. I think I said "I need to go home." Or something like that. I didn't know what was happening to me; all I knew was, I could not face another day, or even another hour, at the telephone company. Then I did the bravest thing I had ever done as a wife.

I told the instructor, "I'm sorry... I'm so sorry... but I've got to drop out of the class. I've got to give up the job."

When I left the building, my insides were trembling. I had committed an inexcusable act. How would I tell Jim what I had done?

The heavy brass doors of the Kresge building swung open onto the Nicollet Avenue Mall and a gust of fresh air caught me full in the face and filled my starving lungs.

Jim will be crazy upset when he finds out. We need the money. What will I tell him? What can I say?

Outside of the trapped stagnant air of the old building, the open air flowed across my face and I took huge gulps of it. I realized with a thrill of both fear and elation, *I'm not at the Telephone Company any more.*

I came to the corner, Dayton's department store. I had worked nights at Malley's in New Haven, so I knew the salesgirl job. I fumbled in my purse for a crumpled Kleenex and wiped any tear-smudged mascara off my face, then I walked into the store and asked directions to the employment office. I went to the elevator, straight upstairs, and filled out an application. Within an hour, I got the job.

I didn't know what I would do next, or how I could face Jim. I had taken a wild leap on instinct, but my instincts were very clear. With the assurance of the new job, I felt a rush of near-euphoria and a strange sort of strength, and yet I felt very calm. It was a new feeling, and I liked it.

There was no hurry to go home. Jim would still be at he school. I had a little money he had given me for bus-fares, so I went into a sandwich shop. I sat at the counter and had a hot pastrami and pepper cheese on rye, and I celebrated. I didn't know, at the time, exactly what I was celebrating, but it was my first brave step toward reclaiming my right to a life. For the first time in a very long time, I felt like a person again, and it was a good, good feeling.

In the afternoon when Jim got home, my insides started shaking again. With a quaver in my voice, I told him what I had done. We both knew that the department store job would pay a lot less money than the Telephone Company. The look on his face was one of surprise, but something more shocking was still to come.

I had made my plan, and emboldened by the pastrami and pepper cheese, I had gathered the courage to speak it. I told him with the steadiest voice I could muster,

"When I give you my paychecks, I want the stubs, for receipts, so I can keep track of the money. When the fishing equipment is paid off, I'm going to quit the job."

I felt my cheeks flush, but I stood firm, facing him. He looked startled, as if I'd thrown a bucket of ice-water on him. There was a long moment of silence, and then, he agreed to the deal.

In the dim flickering fluorescent lights of the telephone company training room, something changed. I changed. When I broke down, something broke through, and now I have blundered upon a truth far beyond its surface worth: I have a choice.

The salesgirl job was pleasant and even fun. Just before we left New Haven I had cut my long hair and given myself a chic Sassoon-like style, and now, because I looked young and trendy, they put me in the "Out of Sight" shop," a little section tucked into a corner of the first floor. One wall of it was the street-side display window, so that anyone walking by on the sidewalk could see in. It was filled with flower-child paraphernalia and gifts, Carnaby-Street-style clothes, and posters of the Beatles and the Rolling Stones. The Beatles had discovered Indian music and meditation, and the shop cashed in on the trend by selling cheap treasures from India. Tambourines, little boxes in bright colored lacquers, dresses and blouses embroidered with tiny mirrors. There were sticks of sealing-wax and seals, hash pipes and rolling papers, and all things psychedelic. There were huge colored-glass vases as big as umbrella stands filled with peacock feathers or giant fantasy-like paper flowers. In the background music played, "Lucy In The Sky With Diamonds."

Now I had a little money of my own, drawn from my paychecks. I designed and sewed some new clothes for myself. I began to enjoy life again, an identity was beginning to quietly grow back, just as my fingerprint had grown back, even after being crushed-off in the bathroom door by my brother when I was 10. The sense of my *Self* was growing back too. Maybe a life, for me, could be possible again. I had begun to dare to make decisions for myself. The day I refused to be swallowed up again in the soul-crushing gloom of the telephone company, I walked out of the Kresge Building into a different take on life.

After Jim's fishing gear was paid off and I didn't have to go to the job anymore, I spent whole days reading while Jim was teaching at the Art Institute. I invested my time in studying, thinking, and healing myself. The long depression was lifting, and my mind was returning. My self and my soul slowly were coming back together, back to life.

The more awake my mind became, the more I began to realize the truth of our relationship, and philosophically at least, I began to accept it. The more I accepted it, the less dependent I felt on Jim and the less indebted to him. I had done a lot for him; I had gotten him through a hard time in his life. I didn't owe him all that, and now I owed myself a lot. Now he didn't need me as much as before; he had a job and good friends. My burden of responsibility was lifting.

Things seemed better. Jim was teaching painting, life-drawing, and design at the College. He was happy. He didn't rage very often now. He was well-liked and at ease. He and Joe were great friends and my friend Susan was seriously dating Joe, so the four of us went together to art show openings at the Walker Art Center, performances at the Guthrie Theatre, fishing, and even camping.

The first winter came, so different from the ugly East Coast winters. Here the snow was fresh and clean and dry. We took day-trips into the farmlands, where landscapes transformed magically into perfect pristine counterpanes of white. Small family homesteads dotted the countryside with little wood-frame houses set way back from the road. I loved them because they reminded me of car rides in the country when I was a kid in Texas, in Daddy's old green DeSoto. Now, just like then, we weren't going anywhere.

We took drives for the visual delight of them. We were sightseers escaping the city, wandering vagrants with no destination, landscape painters mentally measuring up our canvases and making sketches in our minds.

Each year after harvest, the farmers burned off the dry dead cornstalks to clear their fields for next year's crop. All winter the stumps were left to rot in place; they would not be plowed under until spring when the soil was thawed soft enough to be turned and replanted. Until then, this left rows and rows of little black stalks. When snows covered the fields and laid them out flat and white as a sheet of paper, the short black stalks stood out like dotted lines, and all the landscapes looked like Rembrandt etchings, meticulously drawn in black-and-white with pale gray aquatint skies. The vast fields of stark white were etched in perfection from horizon to horizon with dark strokes of fence-posts, thin black ink-lines of barbwire, and short black hatch-marks of corn stubble.

We're on a one-lane rutted farm road. Fields surround us in an uninterrupted expanse of immaculate unbroken snow. In front of us, a flawless smooth white blanket of emptiness, cut through only by this one road we navigate slowly, the only one for miles, clotted with frozen mud.

Sometimes we see tracks of foxes or cougars in the snow; there are some of them out here, and wolves too. Further north where the human population thins out, there are bears. This land belonged to them first.

We drive mostly in silence. There's nothing that needs to be said. The beauty of the land is eloquent and complete. The cleanness and loveliness of its pure white innocence soaks into my soul. There is a sacredness about it, and a vast feeling of peace. We are moving as if on an infinite sheet of paper, writing out our lives upon it.

When it was Spring and nearly a year had passed, I was coming out of my darkness and relaxing into the new life. I had read zen books, re-read Henry David Thoreau's book Walden Pond, and written little poems about simple things.

Through the dark years in New Haven, the empty page had been my therapy and my confidante. I had confessed my feelings in secret poems that I showed to no one. After we moved to Minneapolis, I continued to write, encouraged by letters from my friend and mentor, Peggy, the first person ever to see my poems. We had remained close friends even through several years and many states apart.

In Minneapolis now, things were happier. I decided to gather up my courage and try to share some of my poetry with Jim. Nothing too deep or heavy, just ones like the poem about the poppies on the hillside. Even so, sharing any of my writing, showing Jim this deeper part of myself was a risk for me and a brave step.

Jim had an old reel-to-reel, pre-cassette tape recorder. It had only one tape reel that was reused each time. He and his friend Steve in Port Arthur sent each other voice-letters, mailing the tape reel back and forth. At breakfast I asked Jim if I could use it to record some of my poems for him to listen to. "I'd really like you to hear to them," I said.

He answered, "Sure," or some other one-word response.

After he left for the day, I started to record a tape for him. I worked on it almost all day, redoing each poem till it sounded as good as I could make it. I finished as the sun was going down. That evening when Jim came home and I was making dinner, I told him, "Today I made a tape of some poems I wrote. Would you like to listen to them?"

"Okay," he said, "Maybe later. After dinner." And he sorted through the bills and junk mail without looking up.

"I really want to know what you think of them, Jim. This is kind of important to me." I tried to say it earnestly but without sounding needy. "Okay," he said.

After dinner while I started the dishes, he went into the living room and turned on the tape recorder. I could hear his voice over the splashing and clinking as I washed the plates. I stopped and listened, and froze in shock. He was recording a tape-letter to his friend Steve, chatting, making small talk, and *taping-over the poetry*.

I had worked all day to get the words just right without a tremble in my voice that might give away how much this really meant to me. Now it was all being erased, while he recorded a rambling letter to his buddy. I sat down at the kitchen table, paralyzed.

I had told him "This is really kind of important to me."

"Okay." he'd said, and put it out of his mind.

When I realized what he was doing, I could have rushed into the living room and stopped him, at least from erasing all of it. Instead I remained sitting at the table numb, profoundly hurt and shamed. Only a few tears trickled down my face, then stopped. Like the fool I was, I just sat there.

When he got through with the tape-letter to his friend, he came back into the kitchen where I sat silent. I don't remember the encounter except that it was brief. He was totally unaware of what he had done until I told him. Then he apologized in the usual "I didn't mean to" way, more frustrated than sorry. Whether he was annoyed at himself for making the mistake, or annoyed at me for not stopping him, I don't know. Nothing more was said.

When things like this happened, I knew he never really intended to hurt me. It was always some sort of accident, or he just forgot. But too many times, they kept on happening.

Another summer came and went, and as Autumn came I was getting stronger and feeling less invisible to the rest of the world. I'd made friends at the department store the summer I worked to pay off Jim's fishing gear, and when Christmas was approaching, I applied again and got a job as extra sales help. This time it would be my own money.

All the streets and bus-stops were mired in salty slush-ice, so I asked Jim for transportation. That afternoon he dropped me off, promising to pick me up when the store closed at 10:00 p.m. As we drove past the corner of Hennepin Avenue and 4th Street, he pointed to a music store called "B-Sharp Music" on the driver-side, the east side of the street. B-Sharp Music was a large company and it had two stores at this intersection, a big one for tapes, records, electric guitars and amps on the west side of the intersection, and on the east side of the intersection there was a smaller store for sheet music and wind instruments. The smaller one was where, reaching his arm out the car-window, Jim pointed for me to wait for him when I got off work. So I did, unquestioningly, as always.

At the end of my shift I walked to the music store at the corner. At mid-December the temperature was about 10° below zero. I was wearing a light coat, a short skirt and sweater and indoor shoes with nylon stockings which did nothing to protect my legs and feet from the cold. I watched for him from inside the glass door of the music store until it closed at 10:30. Then I had to wait outside. It was terribly cold.

The other store, diagonally across the intersection, was brightly lit and still open, where I could have waited inside, but I didn't dare leave the place where Jim told me to wait, so I shivered and waited. The streets were emptying and the cold was getting intensely painful. My feet in those little indoor shoes hurt the worst.

More than an hour went by. As I waited, I began to feel the old fear again, that he had forgotten me. There was no pay-phone near me, and it wouldn't have helped anyway, since I didn't know where he would be. I didn't dare leave, for fear he would come and I'd miss him. He never came.

I don't know how long I waited. I was fighting back my hurt and rage, getting angrier as the agonizing minutes went by. *How can he do this to me?*

The pain from the cold was fierce. My feet and legs went numb, and yet they still ached horribly. The streets were almost empty now. I reached the point where I could not stand it any longer.

I left the corner. I stumbled four blocks to the bus stop that would take me to my neighborhood and I waited for the bus. When it came, I climbed aboard grateful for the weak drafty warmth on the long ride home to Northside. There I got off and walked unsteadily the two more blocks of rutted icy sidewalks to our house, and shakily climbed the stairs. My shoes were wet, my feet were nearly crippled with pain, and my whole body was cold to the marrow of my bones.

When I came through the door, Jim jumped up with a

look on his face that I cannot describe. His first words were not "I'm so sorry" or anything like that. I remember exactly what they were:

"Where were you?" he blurted out. "I thought you were dead!"

I was angry and tired, shaking from the cold, and couldn't feel my feet, my face, or my hands. I didn't even look at him. I kept on walking, shuffling to the bathroom down the hall.

"I was standing on the corner, right where you told me to wait." My voice was flat and emotionless. *"Where were you?"* That was all I said, but he could see that I was angry. I didn't even ask him why he hadn't come. I was beyond that. I was so tired, so cold, and I didn't know it yet, but my feet were damaged from frostbite.

I drew a tubful of hot water and with fumbling fingers I stripped off my clothes, dropped them on the floor, and immersed myself into the blessed warmth of the water. As my toes began to thaw, the pain became amazingly worse.

I stayed there a long time, and he let me. I refilled the hot water and stayed in the tub until I was finally warm again. When I came out, I was still sullen and unspeaking. He stammered some sort of justification:

"I drove past the corner a whole lot of times," he said. He knew that this downtown area after dark was a pick-up strip for prostitutes. Apparently after "a whole lot of times" and not finding me, he had panicked and called the police.

"A whole bunch of people and the police were looking for you" he said, "we were looking in all the back streets and alleys..." He sounded remorseful, as if he had really feared I might have been abducted or assaulte.

"We looked all over," he insisted.

"WHEN?" I said, openly angry now. "WHERE? I was standing right there! Outside on the sidewalk in plain sight!"

And I wondered in bitter silence, *How could "a whole bunch of people and the police" not see me? Or did they not look till hours later, after I finally left the corner? Or was that whole story not even true? Did he just forget? Again?*

"I was standing right there on the corner where you told me to wait," I said. "For nearly two hours I was watching for you. I never left the corner, right in front of the store. How could you not see me?"

No answer. He looked baffled. I turned away.

At 10:00 there had been a lot of traffic with Christmas shoppers going home. I watched the street for his white Ford very attentively, standing in front of the store where he told me to wait. There was no way he could have driven by without seeing me standing there, especially after 11:00 p.m. when the traffic thinned out to nearly none. The truth seemed perfectly clear: he had not looked at all.

I went to bed and went to sleep. That night he didn't rape me. He didn't touch me. He didn't dare.

I don't remember how it played out in the next few days, but neither of us ever spoke of it again. Unlike all the other times, that night I had complained. He knew I was angry, and it was unusual for me to show it. He must have known he had seriously messed up this time, and he was obviously feeling uncomfortable about it.

He didn't apologize. He never said "I'm sorry." I'm sure he was sorry that it had happened, but he didn't take any responsibility for it. If he made any gestures of regret or concern, I didn't hear them. Nothing could make this okay, and there was a monumental empty space between us.

The story about the police looking for me "in all the back alleys" was bizarre, but Jim had never been a liar. The only explanation I could imagine was that maybe he forgot where he told me to wait, and all the times he drove by looking for me, he never looked at that corner, where he had stretched his lanky arm out the driver's side window to point out so clearly. Maybe he only looked at the other store, the big brightly-lit one that was still open, where I would have loved to be, warm and safe inside.

Four of my toes were frostbitten. They ached horribly at first and hurt intensely for weeks. The toenails turned black and finally fell off. The new nails grew back rough and corrugated, and would never fully reconnect to the nail-beds because of the scar-tissue.

That night was a breaking-point that could not be fixed, forgotten, forgiven, or explained-away. Something between us had splintered-through, had broken like the center-beam of a building, the one that holds the whole thing up. This time, that part had been damaged more than it could ever be repaired.

It wasn't the frostbite that damaged me the most, it was that same old injury-by-default-thing. *He forgot.* He didn't care enough to do a small thing for me, and once again, I had found myself in the victim-martyr's role that I hated. *That was what I could not forgive.*

17: Jim and Joe

Jim's new best friend Joe was a colorful character with a great large loud personality and a sense of humor to match. Everything about Joe was big, including his six-foot-four ample body and his cheerful kindhearted nature. He was the first person who ever called me Victoria. He said it was "charming."

Joe was a storyteller and a folksy philosopher, though I don't think he knew it. He loved to observe life and people. He told us tales about how he used to hang out in pool halls when he was in high school, playing 8-ball with "the old guys" at a gritty SouthSide Chicago bar called the Blue Star.

"Those old geezers could tell you some stories," he said. "Some of 'em worked in shipyards or served in the army duckin' bullets in W.W. II." Joe respected the "old geezers" and I think in a way, he loved them. "They were really wise, those guys."

They probably enjoyed telling him their stories as much as he enjoyed hearing them. "They know they ain't goin' anywheres," Joe said. They must have appreciated his respect and his youthful enthusiasm, because they taught him the insider tricks and skills of 8-ball and snooker that only the old guys know.

When Joe came to Minneapolis and found an apartment, even before he got furniture he bought himself a pool table. There wasn't enough space for it, so when Jim and Joe played eight-ball, they gave nicknames to the tricky shots, like "the venetian-blinds shot" because the end of the pool cue hit the dining room window and laughter blended with the clacking of pool balls. Susan knew how to play pretty well, but mostly she and I just "let the boys do their thing."

Joe loved life. He made a habit of enjoying things. He celebrated an experience like a theme-park ride. He regaled us with jokes and improvisations about Midwestern fishing, farmers, and a variety of Wisconsin cheese-jokes and cow-jokes. He enjoyed the customs and culture of the rural Midwesterners. I guess after life in the big city of Chicago, he was fascinated with it all, especially the fishing. His enthusiasm reeled Jim into it too, and Susan and I usually went along on their local fishing trips to the lakes around Minneapolis. We rented a rowboat and bought some bait at the edge of any lake, and off we went. Susan and I didn't care so much about fishing, so sometimes we just dawdled in the rowboat getting a tan.

The boys always caught a good mess of croppies and at the end of the day we came back to Susan's place and fried up huge platters of the tasty little fish, crisp in brown-crusty beer-batter. We made boiled baby potatoes with butter and parsley and a big bowl of coleslaw, stocked up plenty of cold beer, and invited friends over. Those were great times.

Susan was an outdoor girl, born and raised. She got us out of the city, and once out of the country on a formidable wilderness trip of camping and fishing on the breathtaking Canadian border lakes. The area where we went was so remote that it could only be reached by traversing three lakes and two overland portages, carrying the canoes, the tents, the food and gear - everything - on our backs down a barely-visible narrow path through underbrush to the next lake. Then we had to reload the canoes and paddle across to the next landing, unload the backpacks and gear and carry all of it to the next lake. Three lakes into the wilderness, we set up our camp at the edge of Rose Lake.

Susan had spent many of her young summers at her grandfather's lodge in Grand Marais Minnesota, a town of less than 1,000 residents, not counting summer sportsmen, on the North Shore of Lake Superior. He was a guide for sports fishing trips into the two million acre wilderness of the Canadian National Forest that connected Canada to Minnesota by the border lakes of Ontario.

One resident of these lakes, most celebrated of fighter-gamefish, was the Muskellunge. A Minnesota Department of Fish and Game pamphlet said:

> "The Muskie is one of the largest and most elusive fish that swim in Minnesota. A muskie will eat fish and sometimes ducklings and small muskrats. It waits in weed beds then lunges forward, clamping its large, tooth-lined jaws onto the prey, then gulps down the stunned or dead victim head first."

It went on to say that they're bottom feeders and not very good to eat, but they have a relative that tastes better and is less scary, the Great Northern Pike:

> "This voracious predator is one of the easiest fish to catch because it so willingly bites lures or bait. Northerns produce chunky white fillets that many anglers say taste as good as walleyes. Most Northerns caught by fishing run 2 to 3 pounds, though trophies over 20 pounds are caught each year."

Joe was eager to catch "some of those big guys" and on that trip to Canada, to his absolute delight, they were practically jumping right into the canoe– and the skillet. Joe cleaned and gutted them on a rock at the edge of the water. We made a campfire and cooked them up immediately right on the spot, and ate them. Even with the little bits of sticks and dirt still on them where Joe occasionally dropped some in the grass, they were incredibly delicious. We had fresh air, fresh-caught food, and dizzying wild beauty all around us.

The Ontario Border Lakes Region was like nowhere else on earth. Sunlight sparkled on waters as clear and clean as tap-water, and the air was rich with pure fresh oxygen generated by vast forests of delicious greenness and freshened by many small waterfalls.

Traveling through it all was hard work, but magnificent beyond words. Susan was a master camper and guide. She taught the rest of us basic canoe navigation and how to paddle, and I was an eager student. We started out as couples in the two canoes. The men proved inept and nearly useless, so at the first portage Susan and I, with very few words, swapped teams. Instead of couples, it became girl-girl and boy-boy. Then Susan and I glided along in an easy smooth rhythm while Jim and Joe, trying to "muscle it" floundered awkwardly sideways. We streaked past them effortlessly where there were open smooth waters. At the landing we took a break to rest while we waited for them to catch up.

There were rough places with rip-currents and rapids that even with the best paddling technique were still treacherous. That was when Susan taught me one of the most valuable lessons I would ever learn in my life, possibly the secret of victory in life itself:

When the current catches you, stroke like hell, don't stop no matter what, no matter how much it hurts; don't stop.

I was thrilled and astonished to discover how much pain I could actually endure and how much strength my skinny arms could put out, when they had to. The intense pain transcended into something else, a sort of ecstasy of agony. But we made it. We didn't stop. No matter what.

That first year in Minneapolis, Jim and Joe must have had hundreds of colorful, whimsical art-talk conversations.

"Ya gotta have a gimmick." Joe would say, chuckling his big Chicago laugh, "Look at Warhol. Look at Christo. Look at Sera. It's not what they're doing, it's that nobody else is doing that." And Jim and Joe would both laugh. "Once you've got your gimmick," Joe said, "you got it made."

Joe had an infectious sense of humor and a perpetually optimistic attitude. I remember one time when he said, "It's just the gimmick. You could probably soak cotton balls with paint and stick 'em on a board and somebody would buy it."

But he was not entirely joking. Later he did just that– he made a series of collage paintings out of cotton balls soaked in paint and then stuck onto canvas. As it turned out, he would break into the inner circle of the East Coast art world with that technique, and they were wowed by it. A whole lot further down the road in 2004, I read an article in Art In America by Stephen Westfall that said:

> "Perhaps best known for his paint-soaked cotton-ball works, Joe Zucker continues to invent new ways of "building" a painting. Three gallery shows reveal him at his most spirited."
>
> "The homespun quality of his materials and processes reveals, rather than masks, a keen formal and historical sensibility, while serving his devastating wit and cold eye for high-art academicism."

"devastating wit." I could see that. But *"Keen formal and historical sensibility... high-art academicism."* What?

It was written in art-talk. I did not know that language.

The idea had come to Joe at the kitchen table over a couple of beers, laughing and joking with Jim about modern art. That's the way it goes. I'm absolutely sure that many great revelations and brilliant ideas were hatched at kitchen tables.

One of Joe's favorite Midwestern cultural outings was to take "roadhouse-trips" into Wisconsin, stopping at every rural roadhouse-bar along the farmland backroads, drinking a beer or two and enjoying the locals and the polka music on the juke box, then getting back into the car and driving to the next one. We went on quite a few of those roadhouse trips, Joe and Susan and Jim and me. In the beginning they were fun.

Out on the Wisconsin backroads, along the way Jim and Joe cracked jokes, told stories, or lampooned contemporary art trends. The more they drank, the wilder the stories got. Extemporaneous, not entirely authentic, and outrageously funny. The guys yammered and joked about anything that came into their heads.

The downside was, I saw Jim drunk more often. He could be a marvelous clown, but when he drank too much, he turned into somebody else. One night on the road Jim got off onto a tangent about how he didn't like his mother-in-law, my Mother. It wasn't funny. He went way over the line. The rest of us fell into an awkward silence as he rambled on.

Mother was a wonderful person, kind and caring. Jim had only met her twice, he didn't even know her. I was baffled. I don't remember what he said, except that it was surprisingly unkind and he went on and on, even after everyone else in the car knew it was embarrassing me. It didn't make any sense, but he kept it up until finally Joe rescued me by drowning him out and changing the subject with a joke or another story.

On another trip, Jim started making jokes about my grandmother, about granny panties and being crippled and wearing diapers. She never wore diapers! My Granny Vaughn had died when I was ten years old, he'd never met her. Why was he saying all these crazy cruel things?

He was very drunk, and as we drove through the dark, he rattled on. He thought it was funny. At first he got a chuckle from Joe, but it went on for too long, and it went too far. Hurt and embarrassed, finally I said to Jim "I loved my grandmother very much; please don't talk about her like that." But he kept on pushing it. He made another joke about false teeth, and suddenly it reminded me of how my brother had taunted her too.

"Please don't..." I said in a very small voice, "I loved her, and she's gone now. Please stop." I had been drinking too of course, and now I was close to tears. *Why does he do this?*

When his comedy-acts got mean, Jim became like a little boy teasing a small animal. It was stupid and it was cruel, and there we all were, in the car in the dark on some nameless country road in Wisconsin, and I just wanted to crawl away and hide. There was an uncomfortable silence from Joe and Susan in the front seat. It wasn't funny anymore.

Finally Joe's big voice boomed, "Hey Jim, give it a rest, okay? That's enough, okay?"

We drove without talking till we reached the next roadhouse. When we got out of the car to go in, Joe and Susan smiled, but the fun had fizzled out. We went inside and had one round of draft beer. Joe and Jim were joking again, but the mood was not the same.

We decided to call it a night, and left the bar. I was tired, and I didn't enjoy these road trips very much anymore. I think Susan was getting tired of them too, but we were good sports about it, and Susan always stayed sober enough to drive us all home. Joe was a sweet guy, and Susan liked him a lot. She was falling in love with the big guy from Chicago.

Jim and Joe went out to the parking lot stumbling ahead of us, holding each other up. Jim was still ranting about something, and he was angry. First he was shouting, raging, then he was mumbling, then shouting again. Then suddenly he stopped.

Everything went quiet. I could hear faint polka music from the jukebox in the bar, and no other sounds except the crunch of our footsteps in the gravel of the parking lot. Jim and Joe had stopped. Susan and I stopped too.

The cold crisp night air felt good. A pitch-black sky was spread out above us, sparkling with crystal-cold stars, the way you can only see them outside of town in the winter skies of the Midwest. Joe was trying to put him into the car when Jim shouted out,

"I don't know who Jesus was, but I'm not him! I'm not f---ing Jesus! I'm not f---ing perfect like him! I'm only a man!"

Silence again. Even the jukebox had stopped. And then, in a cry of unguarded agony, Jim shouted,

"My father fell down... but I will not fall down!" Then harsh sobbing, then some mumbled words I couldn't make out. All of this could not have made any sense to Joe and

Susan, but I knew what it meant. "My father fell down..." His dad's suicide.

Joe helped Jim into the back seat and I got in beside him. Susan took the driver's seat, and Joe got into the other side. Without a word, we pulled out onto the single-lane blacktop road. All the way home, nobody spoke.

As always, for me a little alcohol was a lot, so I must have fallen asleep relieved that it was over. Susan got all of us back to her place. She put Jim and me to bed on couches with blankets and pillows and kissed each of us goodnight on the forehead. I remember that; it was so very sweet. That was the last one of the Wisconsin roadhouse trips.

Susan loved to dress up and go out to shows and concerts, and there was abundant live music and entertainment in Minneapolis. We heard Jim Crocce, Tom Waits, and Randy Newman before they were well known. One of the concerts we went to was Arlo Guthrie, who had recently hit the charts with his cheerfully nonsensical "Motor-sickle" song. Jim and Joe were not very interested, but Susan coaxed Joe into it, and whatever Joe was doing, Jim was always up for too, so we all went.

That evening we were in high spirits. The music was happy and full of lively energy and Arlo's wry humor. At the intermission, Susan and I decided to sneak backstage and meet him. It was awkward; we were as giddy as schoolgirls. Surprisingly, when we met him he seemed almost as shy about it as we were. It was silly lighthearted mischief, and it was fun.

Back in our seats again, I surrendered to the simple happiness of the music, I let my spirit float on it like birds on a breeze. I let go of everything else, and let it all fade away completely. It felt good to let go. It felt wonderful.

A soft surge swept through me and I realized that I felt *alive*. The feeling rushed through me like a breaking wave of some nameless joy that I had not felt in so long a time that I barely remembered, and I realized: *There is more out there. There could be more for me.* And then something woke up in me that I thought had died. Hope? Faith? *Life?* Something I had thought I didn't deserve to have anymore.

But I did deserve it, and I wanted it. Something on the inside of me woke up as if from a coma, and in that moment, there I was – *awake, alive.*

For my birthday, just for fun, Jim's aunt Norma sent me a set of false eyelashes! In her note she said "Why don't you try modeling? You would be perfect for juniors and college fashions." It was a crazy idea, but then I thought, What have I got to lose?

She said instead of a resume, models usually have a portfolio of fotos. I asked Jim's friend Mr. Zimbroldt to shoot some pictures for my modeling "composite," the set of pictures with a head-shot and some poses in different outfits, like a magazine spread. A composite includes the model's basic statistics: height, weight, hair and eye color, dress-size, and shoe-size on the back of each photo.

I can't say what my motives were, beyond a silly whim. Maybe I needed something in my life, something different, something brave. As an artist I had always pondered what beauty really was. Maybe I wanted to prove that beauty was not as important as I'd been taught. And if a not-pretty person like me could be accepted as beautiful enough to pass for a model, then one of the two laws: the beauty-thing or the not-pretty thing, had to be be not-true. Either way, I would be released from the responsibility for either one.

I knew I had a chance. I was five-foot-seven and 110 pounds, and I knew how to fake confidence with great elan. I'd had a short lifetime of practice already. My makeup was immaculate, because like most Texas girls, I had hidden behind it for all my adult years.

I dressed myself smartly in my chocolate-brown slacks and chocolate-brown turtleneck that matched my deep brown eyes, my bitter-chocolate-brown "Sassoon" hair, and with portfolio in hand, I went to some of the big stores on the Nicollet Mall.

I found the Fashion Director's office. I said, "Hello, I'm a model, and I'd like to show you my portfolio." The woman who was the head of their fashion promotions whatever-it-was looked at my pictures and said, "We'll call you." They did, and two days later I was a working fashion model doing photo and runway.

At first it felt as dangerous as a roller coaster. At any moment they might find out, and all of it might crash. But it didn't. I was nervous but very focused and rational. I wasn't entirely serious about it, but I wanted to see if I could do it and get away with it.

I was a smashing success. I got good modeling jobs at $60 an hour, which was big money then. I did several runway shows at Dayton's, J.D. Powers, and good old J.C. Penney's Department Stores. I did an exclusive private show at the Leamington Hotel for an Italian designer from New York, Lavino Verna. He had come to Minneapolis looking for new markets in the fast-developing midwest. There were a series photo-shoots to promote store events, and lots of pictures of me in the local newspapers.

I had wanted to find out what "beauty" really was. A

concept or a truth? Modeling didn't provide any definitive answers, but it flushed all the urgency out of the question. It was no longer important.

The modeling thing was fun for a while, like a little game. I felt lighter and opened-up somehow. I learned that *by doing the thing, I became it*. It turned out that I was good enough, and better, *I was good*. I had done something implausible but not impossible, and it had opened a whole new question: *what else might I be able to do, and I just don't know it yet?*

Far from any proof of special beauty, it turned out that fashion modeling is not about that at all. You are a clothes-rack, and your job (and *it is work*) is to make the clothes look good, to sell them with your smile and your body. That's it. It didn't make me feel more beautiful. In fact I felt kind of dehumanized, like an inanimate object. Maybe that's why fashion models are called "mannequins," like the dummies in the department-store showcase windows, things for hanging merchandise on.

By the time spring came, I was done with it. I called it a lark, and forgot about it. But it had been my first venture out. I took a chance. I stepped out of my safe invisibleness, faked much more courage than I really had, pretended professional confidence and style, *and I pulled it off*.

As summer was approaching, I began to look again at some of the stray pieces of unfinished business of my life. I decided to go back to Austin and complete my bachelor's degree in Fine Arts at the University of Texas, the one I had forfeited to marry Jim. I figured it was my turn now.

My best friend Peggy and her husband Howard were living in Austin then, not far from the UT campus. They found a studio apartment for me, and fed me at their place several times a week. It was wonderful to see Peggy again, and get to know Howard. She and I had not seen each other since we'd both gotten married. We talked and talked, woman to woman and sometimes soul to soul.

Going back to school again felt foreign now. The old wooden barracks art building was gone, replaced with a modern concrete one. I roamed the halls of the elegant air-conditioned first floor, looking at the student artworks and sculptures on display. I was startled to discover a life-size bronze figure done by one of my fellow students four years ago. The sculpture professor then, Charles Umlauf, was already nationally known, and each year he chose one or two of his best students' works to be cast in bronze in Italy, where his works were cast. That year he had chosen this one. The statue was a standing female nude. To my surprise I realized, *it was me*.

I had posed for it, not nude, but in a bikini, when I was an art student. I was broke, and the art department gave me and a few other students part-time jobs modeling for some of the art classes. This statue by Dan Hawkins was still there, and like all student work, owned by the university's collection.

There I was, forever cast in bronze, with my trademark Italian hairstyle pulled back on the sides and long in the back, the way I wore my hair when I first met Jim.

That seemed like a lifetime ago. I was an innocent and Jim was barely twenty-one with the fine-boned face that hid a stormy and troubled personality. He looked very young and he hated that. He grew a mustache when it was a fad among his artist-friends. I had hoped it was temporary, but hadn't dared to tell him. He has kept the damn thing for all the New Haven Years, even into his new job as a teacher, even now.

Austin was hotter than I'd remembered it, and the little one-room apartment didn't even have a fan. In skin-blistering heat I walked to campus every day to classes and to work in the graphics lab or spend time in the library. The classes were pleasant, but I felt out of place now. At the end of my summer-school semester, I was ready to come home.

Jim flew out from Minneapolis to visit his mom and her new husband in Dallas and to pick me up at my folks house. We would fly back to Minneapolis together. When I saw him, to my surprise, the mustache was gone! The nasty straggly thing I'd hated for so many years was gone, and the sweet face of the man I fell in love with was back. I found myself feeling newly attracted to him, almost as if I would fall in love with him again.

The good news didn't last though, it was just a mistake. He hadn't done it for me, it was a shaving accident. The razor had slipped and messed up one side. It looked odd, so he had to shave off the rest. I told him so earnestly how handsome he looked, and how much more I liked him without it. He had already started growing it back.

But with the mustache gone, and after I had not seen him for three months, I felt affectionate toward him in a way I hadn't felt since before we got married. Seeing the face I had fallen in love with when life was beautiful, somehow sparked an old feeling in me and I thought, *Maybe, somehow, there's still a chance for us.* Some things were different now. I didn't have to work, and he didn't have the stress of grad school. Maybe we could start over again and get to know each other this time. I wanted to try.

Back in Minneapolis, for the first time in years I felt

some real desire for him. Without the mustache his face was clean-shaven and his sensitive mouth was soft and tempting. After being apart for three months, now when I kissed him, I wanted to. When it was time to go to bed I was not dreading it. I was feeling sensually close to him.

In the bedroom we got undressed. When I put my arms around him and he smiled, he looked like the young man I used to know once, the one fell in love with. Naked he went to turn out the rest of the lights. Just before he could switch off the last light, the phone rang in the kitchen. I heard him answer, it was long distance and he sounded happy at first. He stayed on the phone for a while but he wasn't talking much. I waited. I wanted him to come to bed.

I came back out to see what was taking so long. He was standing there, still on the phone, but not saying anything. I wrapped my arms and my naked body around him. He didn't respond; he just stood there listening to the person on the other end of the phone line. Whoever it was, they had quite a lot to say. Jim's face looked serious, even distressed. When he hung up the phone, he still stood there with his back to me. He seemed stunned.

"Who was it?" I asked. "What's wrong?

"It was Steve," he answered in a daze. His demeanor didn't match up with the kind of conversations he usually had with his longtime best buddy.

"What did he want?" I waited impatiently for a long minute before he answered.

Still looking away, he said, "He told me he doesn't want to be my friend anymore." Jim's voice faded as if someone had turned the volume down. That made no sense. Jim had called Steve his best friend for a decade.

"What do you mean? What happened?

"Steve said he doesn't want to know me anymore."

I was more annoyed than surprised. The sensual mood was gone; Jim was totally involved in something else. I tried not to sound angry. "What are you talking about?"

"The slides. I forgot to send back the slides. I really meant to, but I forgot. Steve just told me he is no longer my friend."

Jim walked into the dark bedroom. I followed him. He sat on the edge of the bed and stared down at the floor.

"I don't understand. What slides?" I was impatient. I wanted to go to bed with him, actually wanted to this time.

"He sent me some slides last year." He spoke almost in a whisper and he didn't look at me. "To show me some new paintings he was working on. A couple of months ago he told me he needed the slides back, and I meant to send them. He asked me a couple of times; he said it was really important. I meant to send them, and I looked around for them but I couldn't find them, and then I guess I must have forgot. He had a chance for a one-man show and he needed the slides to submit to the gallery curator. I didn't send back the slides, so he didn't get the show."

The opportunity, the moment, and the mood were gone. We went to bed. We didn't speak. He went to sleep.

I lay awake. The one time I had wanted him, he didn't want me. He hadn't even noticed any difference. That feeling of *maybe*... that had lifted my spirit so briefly, silently descended. It would never lift again.

Two weeks later, my Bachelor of Fine Arts diploma from the University of Texas came in the mail.

Chapter 18: The Storefront

It was three weeks before Christmas when Jim's mother called us from Dallas. She told us very quietly and gently, "You should come now."

Jim's aunt Norma's oncologists believed she might not have much time left, and the family should come soon if we wanted to see her one more time "as you have known her," the doctor said. The cancer was progressing rapidly, and her dying was beginning to show.

Jim's mom bought plane tickets for us. She would make up some excuse to tell her sister why "the kids" were coming out to visit now instead of at Christmas. Norma's family had decided it was best not to tell her how bad it really was, and the doctors had respected their wishes.

The news was crushing. Norma was young, only thirty-nine, full of life, a loving, joyful person. She was always looking for all the fun she could find, and sharing it. She had been my one source of light and warmth in the desolate New Haven years.

We flew to Dallas. In her hospital room, all of us sat trying to be cheerful, pretending she might get better in the spring. Even in her hospital bed, Norma looked beautiful, haute-mode as always, in a caterpillar-green silk crepe jumpsuit with a matching feather boa. She had lost a lot of weight but she was still our irrepressible Norma. To cheer us up, she told cute little risqué jokes that tore my heart.

Nobody had told her and nobody gave it away, but I think she knew. I could feel it, and it felt awful. I wanted to throw my arms around her and hold her and tell her I loved her so much, but I didn't dare, or she would surely suspect the truth. We all sat together, playing our brave sad charade, pretending there was still hope. I sat silent, smiling, overwhelmed with a terrible sadness. I had never told her I loved her, or that she was such a light in my life, and now I couldn't or she would know that something was terribly wrong, something we had promised each other not to tell her yet. We thought we were pretending for her sake, and God, it was so hard. But I knew that she was pretending for us. We were all pretending for each other.

The nurses let us stay past visiting hours. At midnight we left the hospital and walked together down the slippery sidewalk in a dark freezing rain. So far I had managed not to cry. I turned back for a moment to look up at the hospital, at the window of her room. I could see the tiny lights of her little Christmas tree blinking there, and something inside me broke and bled.

Back in Minneapolis I was deeply torn and desolately sad. I couldn't express my feelings of grief and loss, and I could not resolve it in my mind that she could die. It was so wrong. I couldn't accept the truth of her dying. I couldn't comprehend it, and I could not bear it. I struggled with my sorrow.

Jim was silent too; we couldn't talk about it, either of us. Weeks went by and still I labored to understand, and could not, until finally a realization came through to me that gave me a small fraction of peace, if not acceptance.

Even though she is dying, she has been the most alive person I have ever known.

Against all odds, she held onto life till March. Wilma her sister and Grammy her mother were with her when she died. Jim and I didn't return to Dallas for the funeral, we didn't want to remember her that way, and Jim's mom understood.

Norma had gotten a short-shift in life. It wasn't fair. But for the time she was here, she had been exuberantly here, extravagantly here, and extraordinarily here. Norma had been a joyful spirit no matter what life threw at her. She made some mistakes, but she was all about love and joy, and she shared herself as generously and innocently as a child. That was when I saw it, the simple truth:

A life lived fully and honestly is a life lived well. A life lived here and now, not tomorrow or next year. We will all pass from this place someday; it's one of The Rules of The Game. The greatest tragedy would be to have died without ever having really lived. Norma has really lived. Every minute I knew her, she was so alive, so completely and whole-heartedly alive.

My next thought slammed into my head like a bullet:
I am not.

For years I had been collecting excuses to not be alive. *Can't, shouldn't, too soon, too late,* and most of all, *Don't stand out.*

Now in one flash of insight, the invisible shackles of my own making showed, unmistakable, and I couldn't deny them anymore. In that instant, like the quick precise catching of steel gear-teeth, my mind turned. And began its long and difficult ascent.

I've heard it said: "In every ending is a beginning." Norma's death ended something precious and irreplaceable for me, but it was a beginning too. It was the thing that forced me to look again at my own life.

That was the year Chuck painted the first of a series of monumental heads, an immense self-portrait, a reak breakthrough for him. It would be followed by portraits of some of his friends, including Susan.

Joe and Susan got married. They were moving to New York at the end of the teaching semester and he had gotten a terrific deal on a loft to rent for a studio and living space. Joe bequeathed his old storefront apartment and painting studio to Jim. Until then, they would live at Susan's place . We moved out of our cozy apartment on Russell Avenue North and into Joe's old storefront place in a semi-industrial area at the upper end of Nicollet Avenue.

The store itself was Jim's studio, a large open space with a high ceiling and narrow clerestory windows on one side and two large store-windows that filled the whole front wall with oceans of light. A tattered canvas awning blocked the brightest sunlight and shifted it onto the pavement, where it was reflected as clear daylight through the windows. The huge space was flooded with indirect light, perfect for a painter's studio.

In the back of the store the living space was one small room with a low window looking out onto the brick wall of the building next door. The other three walls had only a door to the front room, a door to the kitchen, and a sliding door to a shallow closet space. The tiny bathroom was next to the kitchen. All the walls, painted a sickly yellow-beige, enclosed me with a dizzying wave of claustrophobia.

The kitchen, though even smaller, was not so bad. A stove, an old refrigerator, and the massive round table and chairs from our old apartment were crammed into it. It had a window that offered a precious bit of sky, facing another commercial building with a gravel parking lot that flooded every time it rained. Mornings when Jim left to teach his early classes, I sat down at the table with my coffee and my thoughts in the cramped space next to the window.

On one day like all the others I sat silent, very still, and empty. It had been raining for days and the air in the apartment was chilly and damp. A steady rain was falling from blank sullen skies as I looked out the kitchen window onto grey puddles pricked by needles of rain.

The rain is endless. I am drowning in emptiness. There is something clandestine about this day, this silence, this life I have. Despite the laws of the universe, time has simply stopped, or worse, it has gone on without me.

Rain spattered the glass and tapped on the windowsill like nervous fingers. The sounds of the rain were beautiful and everything else was silence.

My soul floats above me like a vapor and I feel nothing. I am sitting here below it and it casts no shadow upon me.

As I looked out at the gravel parking lot and dense skies heavy as slate, a desolate loneliness flooded over me and soaked all the way through me. I saw the truth, that my life was as empty and featureless as the bleak skies reflected in the rain pools, and something inside me turned.

The truth came, and quietly presented itself. It appeared unexpectedly like a deer stepping into a clearing from out of a deep forest, a momentary encounter, then disappearing back into the dark woods as silently as it had come. When it vanished, I was left with a strange sweet feeling of both gift and loss. *It's time.*

In that moment I knew, *I can't be alive in this place, in this emptiness.* I realized that I must leave. As quietly as the rainfall, the time had come, and I knew it.

I can't say I hadn't thought about it before. I had, but only in a vague way, like a daydream. I hadn't made any plan, only the thought that someday, somehow, I would escape and disappear. Jim had needed me in the beginning, maybe even loved me, but most of our years together were not about love, only need. I fell into the well of his need, and I couldn't get out. I must have needed him too, but it was not in a way that was good for me.

I'd always known I could never leave Jim until I was sure he could make it without me, and even then, I still hesitated. I didn't want to hurt Jim, I just wanted to disappear, to escape the confines of this life that always held me just at the edge of depression. I wanted to escape from this landscape of ugly brown-brick buildings and the semi-industrial neighborhood where we now lived. When I saw my life reflected in the puddles of cold rain, I knew that this part of my life was ending.

I began in secret to look for some way out. I couldn't just walk away. I had no money and nowhere to go. It had never seemed like an option to go back home to my family as a failure in life. That would have made me a quitter, and I was not a quitter. Now if I left, I must do it on my own.

I had given a hundred percent of myself to support the life of another person. He had used about sixty percent of me, the rest he tossed-out like used coffee grounds. The parts he threw away might have been the most valuable parts. That was what finally released me: the realization that God had given me a life too, and a soul, and a talent, and I was wasting them. Something in me wanted to declare it, to shout it out loud – *I am a person too*. When I recognized that wasting my own life was a sin of omission, something internal simply let go and released me. I felt the chains fall away, unlocked from the inside.

The decision to leave came from both a desire for freedom and a profound sense of guilt for having abandoned my own life. I took that as my justification to stop living *his life,* and to look for my own. From the moment my mind changed, I began to change too. Maybe Jim felt it, but he didn't ask. We had never talked, and now I stopped trying to. I started working harder to make as much money as I could so that someday I could leave.

I had been designing and sewing stage costumes for local rock-bands, and custom-made men's shirts and jackets that I sold in small boutiques and a menswear specialty shop in Dayton's department store. Susan's friend Zoey was also a creative artist in her own right, talented at design and masterfully skilled at sewing. She needed money too, so she worked with me to make the shirts and we split the small income from sales. I applied for a state sales tax Resale Permit and opened a checking account.

One morning Zoey and I were in the little back room of the storefront apartment, bent over my sewing machine working to develop a new design. Jim was painting in the big front room studio. About ten o'clock he took a break and came back to where we were working. Stretching out his lanky arms over his head to relax the tightness from painting, he announced cheerfully,

"A cup of coffee sure would taste good." and he looked directly at us, smiling a big smile. I glanced up at him but I continued working. He stood there for a long moment.

It would have been obvious to anyone else that we were focused and very involved with what we were doing. My annoyance began to rise.

Can't he see? I don't want to get up, interrupt my work, and waste Zoey's time just to make coffee for him.

He was still standing there, waiting for me to drop everything like I usually did, and attend to him. I said, "We're in the middle of this, Jim. Could you make it?"

He was surprised. He stood there another second or two as the realization hit him that he could have made it himself in the first place. He went into the kitchen and started the coffee pot. When he came back out, he asked politely,

"Would you like some too?" It was a breakthrough for him, a moment of thoughtfulness.

"No. Thank you," I said, and kept on working.

I didn't know how long it might take to make enough money to leave, but once the decision was made, I had a choice, a hope, a way out. I kept all of this hidden inside, just as I had always kept my disappointments and my loneliness inside. I kept my hope there too.

We had been living in the storefront place maybe a year, maybe less, when it happened. It was not a part of the plan. I wasn't ready, but it happened anyway, at the end of an ordinary day exactly like any other day.

That night we went to bed and Jim began his customary casual rape of my body, the same way he had been doing for four and a half years. And then without a glimmer of warning of any kind, suddenly I was overcome with an immense sorrow. Unexpectedly, uncontrollably, I started to cry, and I could not stop.

I didn't know what was happening to me. My armor had failed me completely, all at once. Feelings that I didn't understand exploded out of me like a thunderstorm, and the downpour came immediately.

Jim, perplexed, stammered, "Is something wrong?"

I could not begin to tell him how many things were wrong, and that I was trapped in them, and that I had been trapped in them for so long that there had become no chance for any other way.

I couldn't speak and I couldn't stop crying. I struggled to control myself. To my horror, I could not. Long, unbearable minutes passed before the ugly choking sobs began to subside, then fade, finally, into silence. Total silence. A vast, empty silence.

I don't remember anything else.

The next day we didn't talk. He wasn't as cheerful and enthusiastic about his painting as he normally would have been. At mid-morning he came back from the front room studio to the small living-space where I was ironing his shirts.

All he said was "Are you going to leave?"

That caught me off guard. I didn't want to say it. I didn't want to tell him. I hesitated as long as I dared. I didn't look at him, I couldn't. I kept on ironing while my mind raced in circles, searching for a safe answer. There was none.

"I don't know." I said. But I lied. I did know.

He went back into the studio.

Our friends had known, long before either of us did, especially our best friends Susan and Joe. When Jim drank too much, his whole personality changed. He could turn surprisingly cruel, especially toward me. From my obvious hurt, our friends could see that something was wrong, and my unsmiling silences had confirmed it.

I don't remember how the next few days played out. Susan was supportive and kind. Zoey offered to share her apartment with me for a while until I could figure out what to do. I remained awkwardly in the storefront apartment during the daytime for another week because our sweet little cat was pregnant and about to give birth. Jim was gone all day at his teaching job, and I didn't want her to face that alone.

Two days after the kittens were born, I moved out. Jim loaded what little I took with me into the back of his car and drove me to Zoey's place. The day I took my life back was unknowingly symbolic: July 14th, Bastille day.

I didn't know where I would go from there, I only knew I had been too long without a life. I knew I could never get back the life I had foolishly thrown away when I left college, and I knew that to leave the way of life I was leaving now required one more sacrifice— tearing away a part of myself and leaving it behind, as an animal will sometimes gnaw off its own leg to escape a steel trap.

I had taken flight blindly, and without any supporting evidence whatsoever, I dared myself to hope I might find a new life that would be better.

Chapter 19: Freefall

At twenty-one I had traded away my life as an artist for the career of wife and caregiver. Now, that too had crumbled into ashes. At twenty-five, again a life as I had known it was gone, this time traded for nothing but free air. Cut loose from whatever foundation I'd had, I stood at the brink of a great void, and I stepped off.

Fading twilight. I long for peace but there doesn't seem to be that for me. Silence, yes, and emptiness, but not peace. Solitude so deep that it seems almost sacred. In the world of people, I can't collect my senses. I feel lost even in familiar places. Things don't make sense.

Days I drift around the apartment until Zoey comes home, or I go to the public library. Or I go downtown and wander around feeling a disconnected vigilance, an undercurrent of fear. Fear of what? I come home again to sit in the dark. Who am I now?

Drawn back again into the feelings I had refused to feel in New Haven, I couldn't avoid them anymore. I couldn't not-feel, I had lost control of that. When the feelings came now, many times I found myself suddenly flooded with the sadness of them. I surrendered to the flow of burning tears that seared my face; I let them pour. I let myself sink beneath dark waves, and die for a while.

Beneath the waves there is a kind of serenity. It's a place I know, a place of refuge. I spent many hours of childhood here. When I sit alone in the dark and cry my heart out to no one at all, somehow there is a great release in that. A kind of calm flows out of it that's beyond emotion or circumstance, beyond anything my mind can understand. I dissolve into my own soul, and there at last, I rest.

Leaving Jim meant giving up Susan and Joe and most of our other friends too. He got all the friends and had all the credit. Even though we had lived on my earnings for more than three years, all of the money had been in his name. The little business with Zoey was my first checking account since college. I didn't have a credit card.

Zoey and I continued working at our designing and sales. This passage was hard for both of us. We didn't know each other well enough to talk about such things. For Zoey, it was harder than I knew. She too had deep wounds that I didn't know of. Like mine, her sorrows were hidden and slow to heal, and I was too wrapped up in my own pain to realize hers.

For me this was a time of selective numbness. I was incapable of feeling any joy, but intensely sensitive to any kind of pain. Tearing myself away from the old life was like cutting my own heart out with a garden spade. The old life had ended before I was ready, and now there was a gaping empty space in front of me: the unknown. Freedom was terrifying.

I saw myself as an absolute failure. The old life was over, and yet I was still here, physically embodied in the same world and the same city. I stumbled through the days.

When the old life ended, I had ended too. Now, whoever I was before, true or false, had ceased to exist. Stripped of my best self-defense– denial, I fell apart and submerged into depression. I had crashed my life, and now I was stumbling through the debris of it.

Zoey worked at the Art Center gallery during the day. I had no job and no prospects for one. I sat in the apartment in a near-catatonic state and drifted through the days as if sleepwalking, or else I took the bus downtown and roamed aimlessly through department stores, looking at things. I didn't buy anything. I didn't want anything. I had no money anyway. With what little I earned through our shirt design sales, Zoey and I together barely managed rent and food.

The Minneapolis Public Library became my sanctuary and my hiding place. I had a favorite corner in the poetry section where hardly anyone ever came. When I was a child in Dallas, the library had been a natural refuge where I felt happy and safe. Now again I found a place of my own. I read mostly poetry. I looked at magazines like The Ladies Home Journal, Harper's Bazaar and Vogue and tried to imagine the lives I saw in the pictures. I could not.

Sometimes without any warning I was overcome with intense sorrow. It surged up suddenly, and when it did, I would burst into sobs. When I felt one of those times coming, I had to run and hide. In the library I rushed to get to the restroom before I disintegrated into paroxysms of sobbing, because once it started, I couldn't make it stop.

In shame I hid in one of the stalls and smothered my face in my hands to suffocate the sounds. I held my breath, and held onto myself until it passed, until I could regain myself. Then I washed my face and slipped invisibly back into the world again.

It was a day in the library when I saw it. All of a sudden there it was, and it was so simple.

He raged. I cry. It's the same thing.

It was the only way either of us could express what could not be expressed that did not expose its secrets. A way that vented the pain without revealing the cause. A way to cope with the shame without admitting it.

Jim raged, and I weep. That was how it had to be for him, and this is how it has to be for me. Okay Vic, you can have this. Go ahead and express whatever emotion still works. Maybe it's a safety-valve to blow off some of the pressure from the inside to the outside. Maybe when you get better, you won't need it.

Months went by like blank pages. I continued to feel very lost, disconnected and unstable emotionally, but I didn't know what to do. I considered the possibility that I might be losing my mind.

I wrote to Peggy. I knew I could confide in her, even my worst weaknesses, and she would not condemn anything honest in me. I told her what I was going through. She quickly wrote back:

"There are people who will help, but you have to ask for it. Look up your County's Mental Health Department in the phone book, and go there." She said "Anyone can go there, and if you have no money, they will help you anyway." I found the number and phoned; they said I could come.

I presented myself at the reception desk of the dingy office on the fourth floor of an old building downtown, an annex of the County Hospital. The stagnant air in the waiting room smelled of dirty rain-wet clothes and stale cigarette smoke. I felt dizzy and sick to my stomach. The woman at the desk gave me some forms to fill out. I sat down and read them carefully, trying to make sense out of them. I filled out what I could, left the rest blank, and returned to the desk.

"Do you ever have thoughts or plans of suicide?" she

asked, as calmly as if the question was perfectly normal and routine. I hesitated. I wasn't capable of thinking as clearly as that, to actually have any plan for anything at all. I stood there blank-faced and emotionless. "No." I said.

The Hennepin County Mental Health Services signed me up for an appointment in a few days with a psychiatrist. My need was considered "acute," but not serious enough for the locked ward. The ward was the last resort for those who might harm themselves or others. I would be seeing the shrink at the clinic twice a week. I complied.

I had never smoked. I started smoking. I smoked until my throat was raw, and then I smoked some more. Maybe I did it to hurt myself, maybe it distracted me from my greater pain, I don't know, but I got through the days and weeks, just surviving, nothing more.

I filed for divorce. The County Legal-Aid Service told me what to do. I didn't ask for alimony or support. I should have, after all, I had supported him. But I wanted it to be over, so I asked for a single sum that I thought I could live on for a year. It was absurdly little, not nearly enough, but I didn't know any better. I hadn't had access to any money for four and a half years. When Jim got the divorce papers, he called me. He was angry, and he said he wanted to see me. I felt my stomach wrench with anxiety.

"Please don't come," I pleaded. "There's nothing to talk about now." I don't remember what else we said. He called again a few days later and this time he was more calm. He wanted to contest the divorce. I begged him not to.

"Please don't, Jim," I said with a practiced voice that I hoped would sound unafraid. "Please don't make it harder." He was vague. I don't think he wanted me, it was just his pride telling him he ought to put up some sort of a fight.

Zoey offered to be my witness at the divorce hearing. It was a standard procedure in Minnesota for any uncontested divorce. If the spouse did not appear at the hearing, the divorce was usually granted automatically.

Zoey and I went to the courtroom together. The docket was full and we had to wait through several other women's cases. Each testimony was obviously the tip of the iceberg of the real story. One witness described how the husband spent all his time with his Ford Mustang instead of his wife.

I waited anxiously, afraid Jim might show up even though I had begged him to let me go and I had sworn that there could be no return. If he came to the hearing, that would mean it would not be over. I sat in the courtroom waiting, shaking a little, taking rapid shallow breaths.

Zoey was going to testify to "mental cruelty," which seemed to be a common reason women in Minneapolis sued for divorce. I didn't know what she was going to say, but she told me, "Don't worry. It'll be okay."

Zoey testified that I had been psychologically mistreated by my husband, and she described an incident I had entirely forgotten. It happened one night when she and I had been working together all day and she had stayed for dinner.

"Her husband ridiculed her cooking," Zoey said. "He found a hair in the fried chicken crust, and he stood up, waving the chicken around, making jokes and laughing." As she told the story, it sounded even more superficial than the Mustang story, but I'm sure the Judge knew it was not. Then I remembered it, and even the night it happened. Jim had done a whole comedy routine. I think Zoey had said, "Well, it sure tastes delicious!" in an attempt to rescue me, but Jim continued on and on. I had been horrified, and she had sat squirming in her chair with embarrassment.

Now as she talked, I remembered the piece of chicken Jim had held up to show everybody, a chicken thigh. I could see it again clearly, even the offending hair itself. A tiny light-brown hair, about a half-inch long. My hair was dark bitter-chocolate brown. *It was his hair.*

Jim kept his promise and didn't show up. My divorce was final December 8, 1968, five years after the wedding day. I stopped smoking.

I took back my maiden name because it was my name, and I didn't want anybody else's. I took back my name as a statement of taking back my life. I had stayed with my marriage until there was absolutely nothing left for me, then I stayed years more. I had stayed until he got through school, and then until he got his first teaching job, and then I stayed until I paid off his credit card debt. I had stayed until I was sure he could make it without me.

Then I had left blindly but with a total resolve, driven by an inner imperative that I did not fully understand. It was my own choice and my soul's necessity, and yet, when I broke away I was shattered at losing the life I had known, because I had nothing else to replace it.

I didn't take much with me. A sleeping bag, and the old Framus guitar Bob and Dotty had given me that first week we were in Minneapolis when they were moving out and we were moving in to "the teacher's-life." I kept the old Aries camera Jim's friend and mentor Joe Zimbroldt had given him and Jim handed down to me.

The passing on of the camera was a genuine gift on Jim's part. It was the only thing he ever gave me that I didn't pay for, except a little Mexican pottery owl he had given to me a few days after we were married. He'd said its hand-painted dark eyes made it look like me. When I woke up disheveled one morning, in a rare tender moment he had called me "Raggedy Owl." Through all my travels and the many possessions that have come and gone in my life, somehow I still have the little pottery owl.

When Zoey and I got back to the apartment it was late afternoon. She gave me the gift of privacy. I went to my room and stared at the cardboard boxes that contained my possessions, remnants of my old life. It seems incredible now, but somehow I still had my wedding album and a packet of letters tied with a blue silk ribbon, the ones Jim had sent to me after he moved to New Haven and I was still in Austin and we were longing to be together.

I took them and went outside. There were very few air-pollution ordinances then, and most people had a burning-barrel in the backyard to burn leaves or paper trash. Ours was a 55-gallon steel drum.

There was a smoldering fire in the bottom of it, and when I stirred it with a dry stick, and the fire burst into life. I untied the ribbon, and one by one I dropped each letter into the eager flames of the burning-barrel. Hypnotized by the fire, I watched them burn.

Then the wedding album. I removed the happy pictures of what had become such a sad story. I burned them too. All except for two small photos. One was of my birthmother Ann in her pretty blue dress with the mother-of-the-bride corsage that Mother had so kindly and graciously given to her. The other one was of Daddy and me together just moments before the ceremony. On my father's beautiful face is the tenderest look I have ever seen on any man I've ever known. He is about to "give me away" and I am about to make the first great mistake of my life.

When I came back inside, the sun was going down. I

looked at myself in the bathroom mirror and asked the face that stared back at me, *Who am I ?*

The last intense deep-gold of sunset poured through the bathroom window and dramatically flooded one side of my face with a dazzling light that was almost blinding, while the other side was in darkness. It was one of those singularly rare images that photographers call grab-shots, when the opportunity is only there for a few seconds. I went for the little viewfinder camera and came back again. Bracing it against my chest, I pointed it at the mirror, and clicked the shutter.

And the face in the mirror said to me, *This is who I am now. I am not who I was.*

In my therapy, the County psychiatrist asked if I did drugs or marijuana. I said no, I never had, which was true. He wore horn-rim glasses and a grandfather-cardigan sweater buttoned down the front, striped brown and gray. I called it his psychiatrist sweater. He smoked a pipe. I thought he tried very hard to look like a psychiatrist.

He didn't seem to be much help. My clinical depression was so deeply entrenched, it would be slow-moving and reluctant to let go. He didn't take notes. I thought shrinks took notes like on TV.

I don't remember these sessions. Most of the time I thought he wasn't listening anyway. Psychotherapy, or whatever that was, did not feel profound or productive for me, but it may have saved my life. It didn't glue together the shattered pieces, but it gave me someplace to go twice a week. Eventually I came to realize that other people can't really help you; they can only try, and their contribution is simply to be there for you and want to help. Ultimately you've got to do the healing yourself, and it takes time.

I resented that truth. And I resented this dour gloomy man, though I shouldn't have. I still don't know for sure if he helped or not, but I do know that for things like this, in the beginning the increments of growth and healing are almost imperceptibly small. People like me who are stumbling through a painful and uncertain life-situation want some all-powerful Dr. Wizard to tell us the secret of how to make our life work. Nobody knows that secret.

The failure of my first love and its magnificent idealistic commitment had shattered my faith in almost everything I believed in up until then. I had been a good wife. I had stopped living my own life and invested everything into his, because I believed I should do that. Now in leaving his life, I had leapt blindly back into my own, which now had no ground beneath it. I had reclaimed the right to a life of my own, but I had no idea how to live it.

I hadn't made the choice rationally, and could not have, based on the rules I'd been taught. The choice, the imperative, had evolved underground and then one day it was time. I might never have found the courage to leave my old life, but I was exploded out of it by an instinctive blind urgency.

Out in the universe when a star explodes, it becomes a cloud of nothing but shapeless energy. And so am I. I have become nothing. I feel like nothing. My self-esteem is zero. I don't even have a self that I can recognize or reach. Everything I thought I knew has fallen away at once.

Recovery would be painful, because as I became more well, I also became less numb. I wrote poetry and emptied out my woundedness onto the page and then I felt a little bit cleaner, a little stronger. I could write in times when it was impossible to speak. I could sit down alone and words would pour onto the paper. Then I could read them and find out what I was feeling and try to make sense of it.

In those lines, I saw that there were two of me. An outside one, and an invisible inner one. The outside one had learned how to survive, but that one was a liar. Only the inside one knew how to live, how to feel, and how to express. I wanted to reach this inner part of myself, and the poetry seemed to hold a way. Even in my bewilderment, another truth was dawning, and I saw it clearly:

It takes more courage to let go than to hold on. While you're holding on, at least you know where you are, and there's a kind of safety in that. When you let go, you are free-falling into the darkness of the unknown. This is terrifying, but this is the way everything begins.

As I stumbled into this new life, Peggy's letters continued to encourage me, praise my poetry and writing, and support me in every way she could. By then, she and Howard had moved to Michigan and he was in art school in Ann Arbor.

Peggy had been my gentle and generous mentor when I wrote my first poems. She was the one person on earth I could tell the whole truth to, and feel safe. Even after our lives had gone separate ways to different states, we had kept our close friendship through long letters. Her letters were truly literature. They were spiritual, philosophical, expressive, insightful observations of life and love.

Peggy and her husband Howard, like myself, were now very far from Texas where we all began. They were living in a small rented lakehouse in the tiny resort town of Keego Harbor Michigan. They had lovingly redecorated it and made a cozy home for themselves and their new baby

Rachel. Howard was working part time and going to school studying art. Peggy wrote to me about their idyllic life and the peaceful charm of the place, and I wrote to her about my fragmented life, my unstable emotions and my shaky state of mind. She wrote back, "You should come to Keego Harbor,"

By a stroke of luck or providence, a new friend I'd met was going to Ann Arbor and offered to drive me and my things in his station wagon. There was no logical decision, I had no plan, but things fell into place. By this and nothing more, I knew it was the next step for me.

I told the psychiatrist "I won't be seeing you anymore."

He said, "Well, I think your house is in better order." That was all he said.

I packed up my belongings once again and I moved to Michigan. There would be more than a new life for me, there would be many.

Chapter 20: Keego Harbor

> The county psychiatrist said,
> "Your house
> is in better order."
> Better than what,
> he didn't say.
> Better than when I first shambled in,
> I presume.
> And so I have come
> without so much as a cup and a spoon
> to bang together,
> to Keego Harbor
> to hope and to heal,
> to spend the winter
> with this somber lake,
> these colorless skies.
> No keys on my keychain
> and few possessions,
> I cast no reflection
> on the water.

In Keego Harbor, time slowed down. It moved gently in an effortless pattern like the little ripples on the calm gray lake. The town was less than half a square mile in area, a gas station, a burger place, and a post office. Most of the lake cottages were empty for the winter, so Peggy found one I could rent, four doors down from theirs.

And so I came, a soul adrift, to live at the edge of a winter lake, and except for these friends, entirely unmoored and ungrounded.

Here my life would become profoundly simple. In the mornings I took solitary walks along the edge of the lake. I passed through the perimeters of the empty lakefront properties, past thickets populated only by squirrels and birds and the occasional raccoon. Every afternoon I went to the post office to see if there might be a letter from my family in Texas or some poems from Robin, the hippie poet friend I'd met at a poetry reading a few days before I left Minneapolis.

Here there was a feeling of no-time. An open-endedness lay out before me, as flat and featureless as the sullen lake and limitless span of empty sky. Plenty of room to think.

For most of my life I have tried my best to please people, to be what they wanted me to be, so they would love me, so they wouldn't hurt me. They hurt me anyway. I kept on doing that until I was twenty-five years old, and now I can't do it anymore.

When I left Jim, I took my life back, accepted the sole responsibility for the living of it, and began again alone. It would take time for the sadness to relent, but when it finally did, I knew it, because I felt a groundswell of *anger.*

It surprised me with its intensity. It was not some old anger, it was new anger. I was not just angry at Jim; I was angry about what had happened to me, angry that I had let it happen, and angry that I couldn't stop it from happening because I didn't realize I could have.

The anger came not as a memory but like the delayed shock-wave from an explosion miles away. The invisible force-field of it slammed into me, still powerful from a distance. I felt the detonation of the outrage I had not allowed myself to feel back then, and just like Jim used to do, *I raged.*

I raged for days. I was consumed with it. When finally it subsided there was a release, a calm, an equilibrium. I felt nothing else but forgiveness, for him and for myself, because we had both failed so badly.

I had married Jim not only because I loved him (though I believed I did love him) but because I thought that being a part of his life would expand and inspire my own. He was creative, talented, and intelligent, and so was I. I thought that we would be partners in life and have adventures together. That was my error. It never happened. It was not a part of his plan. *I didn't see that coming,* it was my mistake.

> Maybe I'm crazy.
> Sometimes I
> sit in the dark and cry
> for no good reason.
> Just because of old mistakes,
> remembering
> how beautiful it could have been
> but it wasn't.
> Wallowing in my own self-pity
> for the years I wasted
> waiting
> for things to get better
> and they didn't.
> Sometimes I wake
> in the middle of the night
> and I have to get up
> and eat bread-chunks in milk
> like mama made for me
> when I was two

and she was still my mother.
Maybe it was meant to be
like this, my education
in life and love,
et cetera.
No I'm not crazy, just mad as hell.
I didn't get what was promised to me.
Leave me alone and let me rage,
the only thing that makes it feel better,
blows it all out,
burns off the cobwebs and rust
of mind-congestion,
crusted with dried up
worthless memory.
After the rage, the sadness returns,
when the mind finally
admits defeat
and the heart takes charge,
soothing itself
with the balm of tears
like in all those old-fashioned
love songs.

The 60's were a wonderful time for music and art and I was in the geographical center of both. Those years should have been a glorious exciting time for me, but instead I had spent them in the lonely shadow of someone else's life.

    I berated myself, *How could I have been so stupid? So docile, obedient, and uncomplaining? I just defaulted back to the victim-martyr role that had imprisoned me in my childhood, the one I hate more than anything, the one I thought I had left behind me. And now in the end, I have escaped back into my own life the only way I know how: by running away,*

When the lake froze over, Peggy and Howard borrowed ice skates for me and one night the three of us skated out across the lake in the dark. There were no markings and no boundaries and the blue glow of the ice and the vast blackness of the sky seemed to go on forever. Every so often there was a loud BOOM! as the ice-layer shifted itself alarmingly beneath us, but held firm. Then silence again, and only the scrape of skates.

Spring came and the lake turned liquid and blue again, everything else turned itself ecstatically green, fed by tempestuous rainfalls, magnificent storms, dark foreboding clouds, loud rumbling thunder, and sky-splitting flashes of lightning that lit up the night like noonday. In the day, powerful forces were gathered up and then thrown down in torrents of sudden hard rain. The storms, so thrilling to watch from safe indoors, were terrifying if you were caught out on the lake in a light canoe, racing the storm to shore.

Sunny afternoons while Howard was at school, Peggy and I took the baby Rachel and Basset hound Lily canoeing along the shallow waters near the shore. Or sometimes I took the canoe out alone, exploring a half-mile or so out. I could see the sailboat races far away on the other side of the lake. From here they looked like toy boats with white handkerchief sails. Along our shoreline I picked cattails to make a flower arrangement for my little lakehouse that was unfurnished except for a kitchen table, two chairs, and the floor-pallet I slept on.

Journal: Yesterday the sky was blue, today it's the color

of pewter. Everything is absolutely still, not a breath of air. A low rolling thunder is mumbling someplace far off and the clouds have been dark and saturated for days. The storm is still northeast of us, a massive front off Lake Superior. When the rains come, they will be swift and powerful, appear out of nowhere, and whip our little lake into white-caps. Now the lake is flat as glass, but I won't go out on the water. Any minute the deluge could start. It will come down hard and pound the earth for days.

Keego Harbor was a refuge, it was the space I needed to bind up my wounds, and the clear span of time for my mind to begin to gather itself back together. In this profound solitude there was a deep well of strength that could be drawn upon, a gift of undeserved grace that soothed the way for my healing. In some unexplainable way, I knew I was made more whole by having been broken and scattered, then sequestered in the heart of the silent winter with a promise of a different spring.

Evenings I walked the edge of the shore alone with my thoughts. The air was so clean and the stars so clear and bright that the damaged parts of me seemed to melt into the night sky. I could release everything that I was before, and I became that beautiful silence. I became sacred.

Solitude is different from loneliness. Enclosed by this cocoon of time, even the simplest things I thought or felt were intensified by a pureness of clarity. I called all of this "my Thoreau experience." I wrote poetry and a journal. Keego Harbor gave me what I needed: sanctuary.

Summer was coming, it was time to look for work. There were no jobs in Keego Harbor. I would have to commute to Ann Arbor, Detroit, or Pontiac. I didn't have a car or much money, and the future was uncertain. Then, abruptly, Peggy and Howard's blissful life took a lurching turn.

Howard's stepfather Martin Mayrath was a wealthy and powerful man, though he gave no special advantage to his stepson. He and Peggy struggled to pay the rent just as I did. In the 1940s, Martin Mayrath senior had been the first person to design, patent, and market the auger, and now Martin junior was the CEO of his corporate empire.

"Basically it's a screw in a tube," Peggy aptly described the auger, a farming device for the efficient movement of grain and other materials. The principle was invented by the ancient Greek, Archimedes. Martin Mayrath recognized its value for agriculture and he designed and built the first commercial augers which could move huge amounts of product to trucks, silos, and railroad cars. It saved farmers time, labor, and cost, and revolutionized farming in the United States and eventually the world. Martin Mayrath junior, like his father, was also an aggressive, hardworking, tough, brilliant "self-made man." His business in Dallas Texas was worth millions.

As a teenager Howard had worked summers in the fields and barns of Mayrath Inc. He learned the business inside and out, and became very skilled at managing tasks and machinery. Martin had mentored him, and then legally adopted him. But the business was not Howard's dream; he wanted to be an artist. It was early May when he and Peggy got the news that Martin was seriously ill, and Howard must come at once to Dallas. Martin planned to bequeath the business to Howard. If so, Howard and Peggy would have to give up their life on the lake and his pursuit of an education and an art career.

Howard tried to decline his stepfather's offer. He had no

desire for an empire. Martin had two natural sons too, but he believed Howard had the mind and spirit to be the best leader for the business he had spent his lifetime building.

Martin's illness was terminal. In the next few weeks, Howard had to make several flights to Dallas. He pleaded his case for the life he and Peggy had chosen, but Martin remained resolute. He told Howard that if he didn't accept the responsibilities the Mayrath empire, he would be cut out of Martin's will entirely.

Howard didn't want the money, he only wanted the good life he and Peggy had made together. He implored his stepfather to let him decline this life-shattering demand. But again Martin refused. Howard could not in good conscience reject his stepfather's dying wish, so he gave in.

As Martin's medical condition worsened, he became progressively less lucid. When Howard first declined the business, Martin had told his lawyers to write Howard out of any inheritance. By the time Howard had agreed to take on the corporation and give up his own life for it, Martin was deemed mentally incompetent to change the will back again. Like a tragic soap-opera story, Howard lost both his freedom and his inheritance. Now he would have to move his wife and baby to Mayrath's factory site in Compton Illinois, a farming community whose primary source of employment was the factory. As the new CEO, Howard would be managing hundreds of workers who were more experienced and decades older than himself. As the top executive in a multi-million-dollar business, he paid himself a starting salary of $100 a week.

Without Peggy and Howard, Keego Harbor would hold little for me. It was time for my sanctuary to end. I knew my best chance of finding work would be in Minneapolis, so I packed my belongings again into cardboard boxes and Daddy's old Navy footlocker, and on the last day of May, Peggy drove me to the Greyhound depot in Pontiac. I felt bereft to be losing her again, but I knew this was just Life playing its game, and all of us were in it.

It was late twilight when we said our quiet goodbyes. The station agent shoved my trunk and duct-taped boxes into the underbelly of the bus, and I got on.

The bus started up with a hiss and a groan, pulled out into a spattering rain and was quickly swallowed up by the falling darkness. Through the rain-streaked dirty window, cheap neon colors reflected brokenly on the wet black streets as the bus rumbled and swayed along. On the road to Detroit I dozed off, but woke again with every lurching traffic stop. Sleep would have to wait for open farmland.

In Detroit the streets were noisy and crowded, full of people hurrying around under the illusion that it mattered. People got on the bus and people got off. A midnight-cowboy dressed in a wrinkled faded western shirt boarded the bus with only a duffel bag and a tambourine. He sat in the very back, and every time the bus hit a bump the tambourine jingled. All night long.

Smells of stale urine and cheap wine hung like a pall over the fetid interior. At brief stops along the route, shadowy figures shuffled on and off like sleepwalkers. On the road again I slumped down into my seat to endure the restless rocking and the fitful half-sleeping night.

Crowded into this suffocating atmosphere with my fellow vagrants, I am utterly alone now. Everybody is. There are brutal encounters with reality here, but nobody speaks it. Philosophy writes itself inscrutably on fogged windows. I can see in the gloomy darkness that everything I thought I knew was not the answer. The answer is out there someplace, running always ahead of me like a shadow on the ground.

Sleeping passengers cough and grunt and snore. We are a collection of stories by Kafka, except you never get to read how they end. We're all running away in slow-motion from the unhappy truths of our lives, to the emptiness of strange streets, the loneliness of the flat prairie lands, and the hopelessness of the cracker-box stacks of houses in shabby clusters along the bus routes and railroad tracks.

As the bus droned on through the night I allowed myself to grieve. I mourned the fact that I had let five irreplaceable years be deleted out of my life by a joyless marriage. It felt like an amputation. I had made mistakes before, but I didn't know yet that there are some wounds that never heal, some that ache for a lifetime like old folks' bones every time it rains. I didn't know I would feel this ache again whenever a tender and melancholy twilight falls, or when the warm summer winds come up from the south and the evenings are lavender and long and sensual. The mistake I'd made this time, I would remember, and the wounds would ache for a long, long time.

In the darkest years in New Haven, some part of me had escaped inward so deep that it could not be reached. I had secretly feared it had deserted me. *What was it? The spirit? the soul?* Whatever it was, it was the alive part of me, the part that once laughed and loved and discovered. Maybe its retreat had allowed it to endure, and it might still stir again.

Returning to the city of my recent past was not a step backward. I vowed there would be no "back" in my life or my vocabulary now. I had learned that I could survive, and

I believed that what had been broken in me might still heal. My spirit had been shattered but was still alive, and more alive than before. Most of the friends from my old life in Minneapolis had been Jim's friends, so I lost them in the divorce. There was no one who would want to see me except maybe Robin and Michael, the young poets from the Wednesday night poetry readings I'd stumbled upon just before I left. Robin and I had become literary colleagues, and through my winter in Michigan we had continued to write letters and share poems. I wrote him that I was coming back to Minneapolis, and he replied that he would meet me at the station.

The bus pulled into downtown Minneapolis on the first day of June in the middle of a tornado warning. Fierce winds tore at flapping signs and traffic lights swung dangerously back and forth above the streets. The air was hot and tense and the sky was strangely dark. Businesses were closed for Memorial Day weekend and people had taken shelter from the storm. The Nicollet Mall was empty.

Robin and Michael showed up at the Greyhound station in a borrowed pickup truck to collect and transport me and my belongings to wherever I was going. I didn't know.

"The YWCA I guess." Instead they took me to Robin's place, a little ramshackle house at the corner of Cedar Avenue and Riverside that was the triangular starting-point of the thriving enclave of the Westbank. Called by outsiders "the hippie ghetto," it was a counterculture village of young and young-hearted people who had discarded the traditional nine-to-five formulas of success in life and experimented with various kinds of something else, especially music and the arts. It was the time of the love-not-war revolution, and while free-love flower- children were gathering on the West Coast, middle-America was only a half-step behind.

The Westbank welcomed me. I camped in my sleeping bag on Robin's living room floor for about a week while his friends asked around to find an apartment for me.

Robin puts some of the dried leaves into a coffee-can lid, and with his fingertips he crumbles them a little bit finer. Then he taps them neatly onto the centerfold of a perfect little square of tissue paper that he has pulled from a clever little package that says Zig Zag on it, and another tiny tissue pops up just like a Kleenex box.

With effortless skill, he rolls a slender, perfect joint. He lights it, takes a puff, and hands it to me. I take a puff. It burns my throat and I cough hard. He laughs.

"Little tokes," he says. "Just take little tokes." And he smiles kindly at how dumb I am. I take another puff, a tiny one this time. And then another.

A few minutes pass, or maybe an hour. We sit facing each other across the small living room. The light in the room begins to soften, and I feel pleasantly drowsy. We don't talk.

I lean back and look at him. He is sitting in a big old-fashioned overstuffed armchair with a high back, so that he can lean his head on it. He closes his eyes.

He is completely framed in the chair like a portrait in a very old painting. As I watch, the image of him begins to flatten, like a cardboard cutout. Then it begins to move backwards and farther away. The chair is still here in the room, but he is somehow moving, farther and farther away. The outline of the Robin-shaped cutout remains exactly in the same place in the chair, but he, his whole body, the real Robin, is receding into a Robin-shaped tunnel that goes deeper and deeper into the chair to some other place, like some other world that is miles from here.

Wait– that can't happen. How can that happen? For a moment I feel a tingle of fear, or something. When he speaks, his voice sounds as if he is underwater. "Are you okay?" he asks. I don't answer. I don't know.

I returned to a city I'd never known before, landing on the west bank of the Mississippi River into a colony of artists, poets, musicians, and free spirits, happy discovering life in unconventional ways. It was a wonderfully alive place to be, and I fell, innocent and ignorant, right into the pulsing teeming heart of it. Like a child in her first experience of the ocean, astonished but fearless, I waded right in, and it felt good.

For the first time in my life I own myself. Never mind that I got here because somebody threw me away. That girl was somebody else, not me. This is Me being Me. This is new, and it is intoxicating.

My new friends found a place for me, a little house at 606 19th Avenue South. I knew right away that it was meant to be mine. It was perfect. An old wood-frame farmhouse that the city had grown up around without noticing, run-down and derelict with peeling paint and rusty nails, not worth repairs, but clean and dry. There was an upstairs apartment whose floors were sagging so badly that it was unsafe to rent, so I had the whole house to myself. The rent was $60 a month, and it was *my place. Mine.* I liked the sound of that word.

The tornado hadn't touched down in Minneapolis after

all. It was just life's little show to mark my leap-without-a-net from the past into the future. Starting again fresh and rested, I fell into an unimagined way of life that would become a daily wide-eyed adventure. I was about to discover a new world.

> The First of June
>
> Yesterday was May
> and I was in Michigan.
> The sun remembers
> the day-shape of me
> laid out on the lakeshore
> flattening the grass,
> and the white heat
> still holds the imprint
> of my slow passing
> through heavy air.
> Perhaps pin-hole stars
> will peer out tonight
> to look for my silent
> shadow walking,
> but will not find it
> there.

I had an innocence that protected me, and a new faith in life had showed up all on its own. The future was wide open with no endings in sight, it was all beginnings. Every day I woke up to surprise and uncertainty. My new life flowed out ahead of me like a river, and I was ready to go wherever it would take me.

Acknowledgements:

I would like to express my deep appreciation
to these profound contributors to the creation
and manifestation of this book:

Peggy Jessup McInnis, beloved confidante and mentor,
who never lost faith in me when I failed.

My Granny Vaughn, who loved me as I was,
and taught me that I was good enough.

About the Author

Victoria Chames is a poet, essayist, and memoirist living in the Pacific Northwest. She began writing after several remarkable careers as an artist, a firefighter paramedic, and a hospital Emergency Room caregiver. All of her stories, essays, and poems are true.

About Darkhorse Press

We are a Small Press in the time-honored tradition of American authors and self-publishers like Henry David Thoreau, Ralph Waldo Emerson, Walt Whitman, and many others. Small Presses and self-publishing have always been a respected part of the American Literature

To contact this author, email:
victory@darkhorsepress.com

www.ingramcontent.com/pod-product-compliance
Lightning Source LLC
Chambersburg PA
CBHW071901290426
44110CB00013B/1229